MORAL REVOLUTION

The Naked Truth About Sexual Purity

KRIS VALLOTTON
& JASON VALLOTTON

FOREWORD BY BILL JOHNSON

Regal

For more information and
special offers from Regal Books, email us at
subscribe@regalbooks.com

Published by Regal
From Gospel Light
Ventura, California, U.S.A.
www.regalbooks.com
Printed in the U.S.A.

Library of Congress Cataloging-in-Publication Data
Vallotton, Kris.
Moral revolution ; the naked truth about sexual purity / Kris Vallotton and Jason Vallotton.
p. cm.
Includes bibliographical references and index.
ISBN 978-0-8307-6602-4 (tradepaper : alk. paper)
1. Sex—Religious aspects—Christianity. 2. Chastity. 3. Sexual abstinence—Religious aspects—Christianity. 4. Dating (Social customs)—Religious aspects—Christianity.+ I. Vallotton, Jason. II. Title.
BT708.V335 2012
241'.664—dc23
2012034131

Rights for publishing this book outside the U.S.A. or in non-English languages are administered by Gospel Light Worldwide, an international not-for-profit ministry. For additional information, please visit www.glww.org, email info@glww.org, or write to Gospel Light Worldwide, 1957 Eastman Avenue, Ventura, CA 93003, U.S.A.

To order copies of this book and other Regal products in bulk quantities, please contact us at 1-800-446-7735.

We dedicate this book to all those people
who have fallen in the battle for their own purity
and are now fighting to be restored.

MORAL REVOLUTION
MISSION STATEMENT

Our mission is to inspire a moral revolution that promotes a culture of love, honor and respect for the generations by providing resources that equip and empower society to wholeness.

Moral Revolution is an organization of radical lovers and passionate people who together, like Dr. Martin Luther King Jr., have a dream of being a catalyst to a global movement. It is our desire that this movement transforms the way the world views sexuality, defines the unborn, embraces the family, values the generations and honors all people no matter their affiliation or persuasion. We have dedicated ourselves to uncovering the root causes of unhealthy ecosystems that perpetuate moral decay and destroy the very fabric of our societies.

We have united under the banner of true love to help provide real solutions for these core issues and not just symptomatic cures. It is our heart-felt conviction that healthy cultures are primarily created through positive reinforcement, intelligent and unbiased education, and honest, transparent disclosure rather than fear, punishment and rules. We believe that when most people are loved unconditionally, equipped properly, informed equitably and empowered equally they are prone to behave nobly.

Why not join the revolution, and together we will make history.

CONTENTS

ACKNOWLEDGMENTS

BY KRIS VALLOTTON

Kathy—You are the woman of my dreams!

Grandpa Bernal—You taught me that I was worth loving in the dark days of my childhood. I will never forget you for that.

Mom—Thanks for loving me and for always believing in me.

Bill Derryberry—Your life is an inspiration to me. Your love has brought me wholeness.

Danny, Dann, Charlie, Steve, Banning and Paul—You have helped to shape my life, my ideas and my destiny. Thanks.

Allison and Carol—Thank you for all the hours that you poured into this work.

Bethel team—Wow! You are amazing! It is a privilege to serve with you all.

Bill and Beni—It has been a pleasure to serve you and to serve with you all these years. I love you both deeply.

Earl—Although you have gone home, your life lives on through me. Thank you for adopting me. I am forever grateful for the inheritance.

FOREWORD

All of Kris Vallotton's books are important and profound. But *Moral Revolution* is the one I've been waiting for him to write. I watched as these concepts and testimonies were being forged in the furnace of ministry where broken people became whole, and the young took on divine purpose with joy. Embracing the standard of biblical purity was never meant to be a punishment for those who serve God. Instead it is another key to total freedom, as *truth makes free*. While many have believed that is true, few have been able to articulate it well. But Kris does. In doing so, he has helped a generation of young people discover the beauty of their sexuality, without compromising its purpose. He also equipped them to make decisions that had the big picture in mind. This is quite an accomplishment when you consider that the young are not known for living for tomorrow.

Books that deal with holiness issues are often harsh and demanding. This one is not. It is compassionate and compelling. In these pages purity takes on purpose and appeal, giving every reader a chance to see the goodness of God in creating us male and female. God called it good.

If you're looking for a book on dating, or simply advice on finding a mate, look elsewhere. It's not that *Moral Revolution* wouldn't help. I'm sure it would. It's just that this book is much bigger in its focus. *Moral Revolution* is a call to war: not a war of words, protest banners and petitions, but a war over thoughts that shape culture and values. It is a clarion call to all who have a heart for truth to step to the forefront in this purity revolution. It is time to move out of ignorance into insight, and from embarrassment over the call to purity to the boldness and courage it takes to stand in the face of cultural opposition. That's how we can reclaim the territory that was taken while the Church slept.

There is enough of the fire of God on the pages of this book to ignite the heart of an entire generation and heal them from the abuses of a failed sexual revolution. The pure are taught how and why to remain that way, while the broken are brought into healing and restoration. God is the God of the second chance.

In his classic style Kris doesn't mince words. His honesty is brutal. His stories are true. And the fruit is timeless. *Moral Revolution* has the ingredients needed to fuel a nationwide change in our perspective on sexuality and real freedom.

Bill Johnson
Senior Pastor, Bethel Church, Redding, California
Author, *When Heaven Invades Earth, Face to Face with God*
    and *The Essential Guide to Healing*

INTRODUCTION

THE REVOLUTION

I originally released this book under the title *Purity, the New Moral Revolution*. I later changed the title to *Sexual Revolution* to target a more radical audience. The book caused such a stir that I began receiving hundreds of emails from people asking me how they could join the revolution. I was stunned by the responses and decided to start an organization called Moral Revolution. The mission of this non-profit organization is to inspire another sexual revolution (see our complete mission statement at the beginning of this book).

The birth of this organization caused this book to take on the additional role of defining our movement. It became the flagship to the revolution, which seemed to demand that we change the name of the book to *Moral Revolution* to create synergy between the book and the organization.

There were also several questions concerning finding a mate, dating and sexual issues that I didn't answer in the original manuscript. I asked Jason Vallotton, who is single and a published author, to co-author the book with me. He added much wisdom and insight to the entire book and also wrote chapter 5 himself. If you read *Purity* or *Sexual Revolution*, I think you will find this new version even more insightful, helpful and inspiring.

WHERE IT ALL BEGAN

In 1987, I was asked by the Trinity County Probation Department to lead a youth group with the kids on probation in our county. I was to be with them twice a week for three months while Probation worked with their parents.

I found myself completely unprepared for these kids. That first night, I had all 37 high school kids playing volleyball or basketball together for more than two hours while I supervised them. I broke up five different fights that evening. I also discovered that these kids had no morals whatsoever. Nobody had ever laid *any* foundation in their lives for how to behave with the opposite sex. It was a grueling and scary beginning.

Half-time came. I had all the kids sit on park benches in that old, rickety, metal gym. As they sat there, impatient and anxious, waiting for the games to start again, I shared the parable of the ring (which I share in chapter 1) that the Lord had given me on the way to the gym that night. I was so nervous I could hardly speak, but as I told the story, their impatience slowly evaporated, exposing hurting and hungry hearts.

Nobody would have ever guessed that these young people were starving for the truth about their sexuality. On the outside, they were hard and crude. They grabbed each other's crotches as they played basketball and called one another the filthiest trash you can imagine. But as I shared the story, they *all* started to weep. At first they were embarrassed and tried to hide their tears, but as my message continued, many of them wailed openly. I was so moved by their response. When I finished sharing, they all just sat there in complete silence. All of us could sense a sort of supernatural awe. A holy hush rested on us like an invisible blanket.

I didn't know what to do. After all, this was not a Christian event. I was partnering with our community to see the broken in our county restored. Several minutes passed. The kids hung their heads in conviction, their tears puddling on the concrete floor beneath them. I knew after that night that none of us would ever be the same. I ended up ministering to those kids twice a week for five years. The group grew to more than a hundred, and that scene on the park benches repeated itself over and over again.

As the years have rolled on, what I have discovered is that it is not just broken kids on probation who need to understand their sexuality. The entire planet is crying out for a sexual revolution! Fathers, mothers, kids and grandparents are all hungering to shake off the slime of perversion and the bondage of religion and to enter into the joy of passionate purity. While the world seems to live in a perpetual orgy and religion relegates the masses to sexual prison, the earth hungers for the truth about sex.

This book was not written to be just another manuscript about dating—it is a catalyst for a sexual reformation. We want to confront the world's sexual root system as well as expose the religious Pharisees who have stolen the passion of true sexual purity. Our prayer is that *Moral Revolution* will rock the planet and rewrite the sexual paradigms of our time!

1

THE PARABLE
OF THE RING

Johnny's alarm rang early on his first day of high school. He stared, bleary-eyed, at the time on the clock and sighed. The summer of 1986 was officially over. As he made the two-mile walk to the new high school, his mind was flooded with questions and insecurity filled his heart. He wondered how he would be received as a freshman after being part of the oldest class in junior high. Would he be liked? Would the older kids tease and make fun of him?

As he passed the jewelry store at the corner of Destiny Lane and Second Street, he suddenly found his thoughts interrupted and his eyes almost blinded by a flash of sunlight glistening on something in the window. He stopped to take a closer look. The flash had come from a ring in the display case. It was nothing he was interested in; after all, he was just 14 years old. But the ring's brilliance burned an image into his eyes and actually made him forget his fears for a few seconds.

He got to school just as the morning bell rang. Anxiously he entered the class, hanging his head and looking for a seat at the back. As the day wore on, he was gratified to see all of his old friends from junior high and to discover that they were all just as nervous as he was.

When he finally made it home that afternoon, his mother was waiting for him on the porch to hear how his first day had gone.

"I survived," he said. "I just hope school gets better tomorrow."

"It will," she smiled.

But the next morning he was even more stressed when he awoke to discover that he had slept past his alarm. He jumped out of bed in a panic, scrambling to get ready. The day before, he had barely made the bell, even though he had left early. *Walking into class late on the second day of school was not an option*, he thought. Everyone would be staring at him and he would want to die. He rushed out the front door, yelling "Bye!" as the door slammed behind him, ran for the first several blocks, and then slowed to a brisk walk.

As he rounded Destiny Lane, the glare of the ring in the jewelry store window momentarily blinded him again, but he was late and had no time to stop and investigate. Yet strangely, he found that while the silhouette of the ring faded from his eyes, its image lingered in his imagination. *How weird*, he thought. *It's like a song that you can't get out of your brain.*

The bell rang just as the school came into sight. Johnny ran the last few blocks and entered the room completely out of breath. Thankfully, several other students came in right after him, covering his late entry. Once again, Johnny saw that he was not the only one who was getting used to high school. As he seated himself, he observed one of his friends grinning at him, and he immediately felt better. Day two was going to be okay after all.

A couple of months passed, and the leaves began to fall from the trees as summer gave way to fall. The mornings were cooler now as Johnny made his way to school. His fears calmed as he settled into a routine. In their place grew an intense curiosity about the ring in the window of the jewelry store that he passed each day.

One afternoon, on his way home, he couldn't take it any longer. He mustered his courage and went into the store. As he surveyed the showroom, he felt instinctively like he didn't belong and felt almost guilty for intruding—a sense that was instantly heightened by the sight of an elderly gentleman in a suit behind the counter staring disdainfully at him.

"Can I help you, boy?"

Johnny approached him nervously. "I would like to see that . . . that . . . that thing . . . I mean that *ring* in the window."

"Which ring are you talking about, sonny?" the old salesman asked condescendingly.

Johnny could feel sweat beading on his forehead, but bravely pointed to the ring. "That one right there."

"That's a woman's wedding ring," the man said incredulously. "What are you going to do with that, boy?"

"I just need to look at it," Johnny squeaked.

"Well . . . all right," he said as he unlocked the security glass, mumbling something about "kids" under his breath.

There it was, finally, glistening under the showcase lights like a star shining against the black of night. It seemed to glow with a crystalline brilliance, beckoning its admirers to look deeper and come closer. Johnny stared deeply into the diamond, and suddenly an image appeared . . . there she was . . . *the woman of his dreams!* She seemed to emerge from the ring like a genie from a bottle. Johnny blinked in disbelief. He suddenly felt intensely alive; every cell in his body vibrated with expectation. He was mesmerized. She was more beautiful than he had ever imagined, or was he imagining her now? It was all so confusing because she seemed so real. He felt like he could reach out and touch her, and unconsciously he did so, reaching in fact for the ring in the salesman's hand.

"What do you think you are doing?" the salesman shouted, jerking his hand away.

"I . . . I was . . . I was trying . . . I didn't mean to . . . I was just hoping to see . . ." Johnny stammered, feeling as if he'd awoken abruptly from a dream. Still overwhelmed by emotion, he suddenly felt so embarrassed in front of the salesman that he turned and ran out of the store and all the way home to his bedroom.

As he ran, he punished himself with every thought, angry that he'd been made so vulnerable by something so unlikely. *What a nerd I am! What was I doing with a woman's wedding ring? What was I thinking? What if one of my friends saw me run out of the store? Johnny, you are so dumb!* But in spite of everything he thought, the vision of the woman of his dreams persisted in his thoughts. Something inside of him was telling him that somehow he had to have that ring.

For several months after that experience, Johnny walked on the other side of the street when he passed the jewelry store so that the salesman wouldn't see him. But even from there, the ring seemed to beckon him, and he started to plan another entrance into the store. He noticed that on Friday afternoons there was a middle-aged woman behind the counter instead of the old salesman, and she looked friendly. So, one freezing Friday afternoon in January, with the wind howling through the empty streets and icy rain soaking him to his underwear, Johnny wrestled the door open against the wind and took refuge in the warmth of the jewelry store. He stood there shivering, not knowing if he was freezing or just nervous. He felt better when the woman greeted him with a warm smile.

"Hello," she said. "Can I help you find something, sir?"

She seemed sincere, and she called him sir . . . like he was a real customer. Johnny stepped forward. "Well, yes . . . yes, you can," he said, in the deepest voice he could muster.

"I would like to see that ring in the window—the gold wedding ring with the big diamond in it. It's right there," he pointed.

She raised her eyebrows. "You have good taste. She must be some girl."

"Girl? What girl?"

"Well, I assume that you're interested in giving this ring to a special someone."

"Yes! Of course I am!" He paused. "I just haven't met her yet," he confessed.

"Do you mean that you intend to give a $10,000 wedding ring to a blind date?"

He was stunned. *$10,000! Holy crap*, he thought, trying hard to look unmoved by the price.

"No! No, ma'am. She's not blind. No! What I mean is that I . . . just haven't talked to her yet," he blurted out.

By now the saleslady was holding the ring under the showroom lights. It was even more awesome than he remembered. His embarrassment faded in the glory of the diamond.

"May I hold it, ma'am?" he asked.

She hesitated. "I'm afraid my boss would probably fire me if I let you hold this ring, young man."

"I am a buyer, not just a looker, ma'am. If I like it, I plan to purchase it," Johnny said, trying to sound professional.

The lady paused for what seemed like an eternity as she surveyed the store. Johnny assumed that she was making sure the old man wasn't around. Finally, nervously she said, "Well, okay. I'll let you hold it for a moment."

Johnny carefully picked up the ring and gazed into the diamond. Once again, the image he had seen before appeared. *The woman of his dreams!* She seemed to be dancing in the fog. He could see her vividly—her skin was dark and beautiful, and an invisible breeze gently moved her long black hair and flowing light blue dress. She was looking directly at him with the deepest green eyes he had ever seen. She was stunning. The strangest thing was that Johnny had the distinct sense that he had seen her before. Her gaze seemed to penetrate his very soul. It was as if she knew him, trusted him, and admired him. He wondered how this could be before they had actually met.

His thoughts were interrupted by a noise. The saleslady was asking him for the ring. He turned to her and said, "I'll take it. I must have it!"

"Shall I wrap it up for you?" she said, obviously challenging him.

"Well, no . . . I will have to put it on layaway for a little while," he admitted sheepishly.

"Okay. We require 20 percent down to hold it for you," she said, playing along with him. "That comes to $2,022.80."

Acting confidently, he reached for his wallet. He opened it, exposing the empty contents to himself but not revealing them to her and said, "It will take me a little while to have the complete down payment, ma'am."

"Maybe I could get the first payment reduced a little for you," she said. "Exactly how much money do you have to put down on this ring?"

"Uh . . . I'm not sure. I would have to go home and figure it out," he said.

"Okay, you let me know what you can do, and I will see if I can work it out for you."

"Thank you. I'll be back."

From that time on, the most pressing item on Johnny's mind was finding a job. His parents were stunned when he announced his intention to work after all the years that they had wrestled with him just to get him to cut the lawn. He even had purposefully broken the pull rope on the lawn mower three times so he wouldn't have to do it. They even offered to pay him to do the job, but nothing seemed to motivate him. But this was different. This wasn't about money. He had seen *the woman of his dreams*.

Johnny discovered that it was tough for a 15-year-old with no experience to get a job. Finally, after days of beating the streets, he got hired at the Clean and Shine car wash down the road from his house. He was beside himself with excitement.

Johnny began a new routine of going to school every day, rushing home, changing clothes and running off to work. When he got home from work, he would do his homework and go to bed late. The next day, he would wake up and do it all over again, and he worked every weekend. It was a grueling schedule that left him no time for school activities, sports, dances or dating. But he reassured himself that sacrificing for *the woman of his dreams* would be worth it. He often lay awake at night, imagining what it was going to be like to give her the ring on their honeymoon. He would sit on the bed with her, tell her to close her eyes, hold the ring out before her face and then tell her to look. He imagined the look on his bride's face, and just the thought of it filled him with excitement. He could hardly wait.

His folks kept probing him to find the source of this change, but Johnny knew that telling his parents, or anyone else for that matter, was not an option. How could he explain to them that he was working his butt off so he could buy a wedding ring for a girl he didn't even know? He knew the truth would land him in the counselor's office. After all, it seemed crazy to him too. But he was compelled to pull it off.

A month passed before Johnny returned to the jewelry store, this time with $250 in his pocket. He entered the store with his heart pounding and his mouth dry, struggling to remember the lines he had rehearsed for weeks. The saleslady was helping someone else, but she looked up and acknowledged him with a smile. The seconds felt like hours as he waited for her to finish. He was worried that the old man might come out from the office and see him. Finally, she turned to Johnny, and he launched into his speech.

"Remember I talked to you last month? Well I started a new job, and I have $250 to put down on the ring." He pulled out a wad of cash from his front pocket.

"I do recall your visit," she responded. "We require 20 percent down on all layaways, but I have another idea I would like you to consider. How about if you open a charge account with us and make weekly payments until the ring is paid for? We will keep the ring as collateral until you pay it off."

"Wow! Do you think . . . I mean, could that really work?"

"I am pretty sure I can get it approved by the manager," she said.

"The manager . . . great." This didn't encourage him. He figured the manager was the man he had met before.

"I'll go ask him about it."

Johnny was tense with fear when the salesman appeared in the doorway, looking grim.

"Hmm. I remember you. I don't know how you managed to convince Kathy here that you could buy that ring, but I highly doubt that you can—or should for that matter. It's absurd for a kid to buy something like that." He turned to walk away.

Anger rose up in Johnny. "You haven't even given me a chance, sir. I will prove to you that I am responsible, and I will pay the ring off before I graduate from high school. You have my word, sir. Sir, you have my word!"

The man stopped, turned to the saleslady, and glared at her.

"I think you should give him a chance," she said.

He sighed in exasperation. "Fine! But you will pay weekly, and if you miss even one payment, the deal is off. You got that? Not only that, but we will keep 30 percent of the cost of the ring as a restocking fee."

"I got it. I won't miss a payment," Johnny promised.

The old man went to his office, shaking his head and mumbling.

The saleslady turned to Johnny. "I am so sorry he treated you like that. I have worked for him for years and have known him to be tough, but I have never seen him behave that way toward anyone." She actually had tears in her eyes. "You should go somewhere else and buy a ring. This is a bad finance deal. You could lose all the hard-earned money you put down on this ring. It is not worth it!"

"Ma'am, I want this ring. I don't want any other ring. I won't miss a payment. I promise I can do this. I will show him that he is wrong about me."

"Well . . . all right, Johnny—can I call you Johnny?"

"Yes ma'am. That's my name."

She reached out and shook his hand, smiling. "You can call me Kathy. Congratulations on the ring."

Kathy drew up the contract, and Johnny signed it. The deal was done, and he left the store with a sense of victory in his heart. Now all he had to do was earn $50 every week.

From that point on, it seemed like all Johnny did was work. And as the weeks became months and the months became years, it became clear that nothing could deter him. He was a man possessed. He had to get that ring for *the woman of his dreams!*

Every Saturday on his way to work, he would go to the jewelry store and make his payment. The old, crotchety salesman would meet him at the counter, and Johnny actually looked forward to giving the man his money. Every payment felt like an act of war. The man rarely made eye contact or said a word as he scribbled out the cash receipt. When Johnny asked to see the ring, which he always did, the man would sigh as if he was being terribly inconvenienced. He would never let Johnny hold the ring.

But as the months went by the old man began to crack, and one Saturday, after two years of Johnny's faithful payments, he couldn't hide his change of heart any longer. When Johnny entered the store, he was surprised to see that the salesman was waiting with the ring already out on the counter for him. "Good morning, Johnny," he said with a smile. "On your way to work I assume." He handed him the ring. "I polished the ring up a little this morning in the cleaning solution. It was getting a little dusty."

Stunned that he had both called him by name and so readily given him the ring, Johnny stared at him for a few seconds before exclaiming, "Thank you, sir!" He marveled at the sparkling diamond. "I appreciate it. It looks great!"

Johnny left the store with a sense of satisfaction. He wasn't too surprised by the salesman's attitude; he had noticed that he had been softening for months. But that day proved that Johnny had won. *I've beaten him, and he knows it*, he thought. *That wasn't just a change of heart. No, that was an acknowledgement of victory . . . the white flag of surrender . . . a sign of a truce.*

The years rolled on, and graduation was just two weeks away. It was Friday night, but not just any Friday night; no, this was the night before Johnny made the final payment on *the ring!* He could hardly wait. He tossed and turned all night long, finally falling asleep sometime in the wee hours of the morning. As slumber overtook him, he began to dream.

There she was, *the woman of his dreams!* She was stunning, pure and innocent as a young child, almost naïve. She danced around him, laughing and teasing him as she moved. Her presence intoxicated him. But suddenly he knew that she was also taken by him . . . her first love . . . the man of her dreams. He could feel her heart beating with passion, her mind flooded with intrigue. This was the first time he realized that she had been searching her whole life for him, longing for his embrace, hungering for his kiss. He didn't want the dream to end, but it began to fade. He couldn't see her face anymore. Then she appeared once again, but her blue dress had been replaced by a nurse's uniform. As he awoke, he wondered about this. *She was still incredibly graceful in her white uniform,* he thought, *but what did it mean?*

He got out of bed and saw that it was already 9:00 A.M., which meant he would have to hurry if he was going to pick up the ring before he went to work. He threw his clothes on and rushed out the door, his mind still captivated by the mystery of the dream. He drove straight to the jewelry store, ran to the door, then stopped and gathered himself before he went in. What he saw next took him completely by surprise. The salesman and Kathy were standing under balloons and a banner that read, "You did it! Congratulations!" There was even a cake on the counter with "Congratulations Johnny" written on top of it. As he moved toward the counter, they both shouted, "Congratulations, Johnny!"

The salesman extended his hand to Johnny and looked him in the eyes. "You are a fine young man. I was wrong about you. Please forgive me!"

"I forgive you, sir," he replied. Everyone had tears in their eyes. It was the best day of his life.

"Keep in touch with us, Johnny," the salesman said as he exited the store. "We are going to miss you."

"I'll miss you too. Thanks for everything!" Johnny left, his cake in hand and the ring in his pocket at last. He could hardly believe it.

Soon Johnny graduated from high school, and few days later he headed for the local recruiters office to enlist in the Army reserves. He knew that if he wanted to go to college he would need financial assistance, and what better way than to spend a few short years in the reserves and reap the benefits of a college education, bonuses, health care and more. He could feel the excitement growing in his heart as he completed the necessary paperwork. The next day Johnny passed the enlistment written test and physical examination with flying colors. It wasn't long before he began his once-a-month weekend training.

But a few months into his training, Johnny's triumph turned to turmoil. He pulled into the driveway of his house and found his mother and father waiting for him on the front porch. The look on their faces told him that something was seriously wrong. He hastily parked the car and rushed to the front porch. As he neared the first step, he could see that this mother was crying.

"What is it?" he shouted. "What's wrong?"

His father, hanging his head, pulled an envelope from his front pocket and handed it to Johnny. It was addressed to him, but it had already been opened. The envelope told the whole story: United States Army. Johnny was trembling as he opened the letter and read it aloud. "Activation notice for Johnny H. Johnson. Report for duty at Fort Irwin, California, on November 15, 1990, at 9:00 A.M."

Johnny hung his head and began to weep. His folks wrapped their arms around him, and they cried together. "They can't do this," his mother protested. "They can't take my only son!" Her weeping became wailing.

"It will be okay, Mama," Johnny said. "I'll be fine, Ma," he said, stroking her hair.

His father said nothing, but his eyes were filled with grief. "It'll be all right, Dad," Johnny said. "I'll come back safely . . . I will. I promise."

A few weeks later, his folks dropped him off at the recruiter's office. There were more tears as they said good-bye. His folks stood watching as the young men boarded the boot camp bus and pulled out of the parking lot. Johnny waved at them until they faded into the background.

Sitting in the bus, he felt like it was his first day of high school all over again, only worse. He looked around at the rest of the guys on the bus and realized that they all seemed to be in the same state. It was a little comforting to know he wasn't the only one who was scared.

They finally arrived at the base and were herded into lines by a shouting drill sergeant, first for roll call and then for the barber's chair. *This guy makes the jewelry store manager look like an angel*, Johnny thought to himself as the barber shaved his head. From there, he and the other recruits were rushed to the barracks by the sergeant, who ran alongside them screaming orders and insults. As they unpacked their belongings into their assigned lockers and readied themselves for the afternoon workout, Johnny was faced with the problem of what to do with the ring. He hadn't been able to fathom leaving it at home, but now he had to find a place to hide it. He carefully wrapped it inside a sock and stuffed it in the back of his locker.

A short time later, he and the other recruits were in fatigues running for miles with packs on their backs. The entire day was a grueling, relentless barrage of exercise and trash talk designed to push them to the breaking point. Some men stumbled and fell, completely exhausted, and others stopped to heave their guts out on the side of the trail. Johnny fared a little better than some of the men, but by the time they finally returned to the barracks, his body felt like a rag doll. He crawled into the top bunk, barely able to get his legs up onto the mattress. He had never been so tired in all of his life.

Four hours later, the lights came on, and the drill sergeant ordered everyone to stand at attention beside their bunks. Johnny slowly lowered his tired body to the floor. His heart was racing, and his head was spinning. His watch said it was three o'clock in the morning. *What could this idiot possibly want with us at this ungodly hour?* he thought.

"Locker inspection!" the sergeant shouted. "Men, open your lockers right now!"

Panic struck Johnny as he suddenly remembered the ring. The sergeant was going down the line of lockers and dumping them out on the floor, and he saw that his was next. He jerked forward to try to get to it, but he was too late. "Stand away from the locker, Johnson!" the sergeant barked. Before he could move, the drill sergeant threw his locker to the floor, scattering its contents everywhere. The sock with the ring flew out and landed at the sergeant's feet. The sergeant looked down. "You have a mess here, boy! Get this picked up now!" Johnny was frozen with horror. "Did you hear me, Johnson? I said now!"

"Yes sir," Johnny said, choking back tears. Rustling his clothes into a pile, he tried not to draw attention to the sock.

"Hurry up! Let me see those socks, boy," he ordered, grabbing them from his hands. Johnny's heart was pounding out of his chest as the drill sergeant put the socks up to his nose.

"These socks smell like dog crap. You got that, Johnson?" He threw them across the room.

"Yes sir, I got it!"

"We're going to teach you how to do laundry the right way, Johnson. Get this cleaned up and then report for laundry duty," the sergeant ordered.

"Sir, yes, sir!" Johnny shouted, saluting.

As soon as the sergeant exited the barracks, slamming the door behind him, Johnny rushed to the other side of the room to retrieve his ring. Its dark blue velvet case had come out of the sock and was lying on the floor in two pieces. Thankfully the ring was still wedged in it. After checking to make sure no one was watching him, he carefully picked up the ring and slipped it into his pocket. It felt fine, but he would have to look at it later to make sure. And he had to come up with a better way to keep it hidden.

Johnny set his locker upright and put all his stuff away. You could cut the tension in the barracks with a knife. Everyone was uptight, wondering what was going to happen next. This certainly wasn't high school. The Army was brutal and cold as ice.

Johnny reported for laundry duty at 4:00 A.M. Exhausted and stressed, he struggled to listen as the private showed him how to use the machines. He was shown a mountain of towels and sheets and ordered to report for breakfast when he had finished washing and drying them all. After he loaded all the machines, he took a moment to inspect the ring and make sure it had really survived its flight across the barracks. He held it up to the light and looked closely. Thankfully it appeared to be unharmed. Then, catching sight of a roll of duct tape on a shelf in the laundry room, an idea came to him. He pulled the liner out of his helmet, took his knife and carved a crevice just large enough for the ring to fit inside it. Then he put duct tape over the crevice and replaced the liner. Surveying his handiwork, Johnny sighed with relief. The ring was completely hidden, and now it would always be with him. *Something finally went right*, Johnny thought.

The following weeks were full of more ordeals and abuse, but the men grew used to it and bonded to each other, gaining strength from the camaraderie as they anticipated their deployment. Nobody wanted to go to Iraq, of course. But the day finally came for the men to receive their orders. The room was thick with tension as the sergeant read off the different places of deployment and the men assigned there. The tension grew with every name, Iraq still unmentioned. Then he paused, looked down at his clipboard and said, "The rest of you are shipping out to Iraq next week. Good luck men. Keep your heads down!"

That night, several men could be heard crying in their bunks. Johnny was one of them. Nobody teased them, and hardly anyone slept much that night. Johnny called his folks in the morning . . . his voice cracking on the phone. His mother dropped to her knees and wept uncontrollably when she heard the news. His father tried to comfort them both. Johnny sobbed quietly as he hung onto the phone in silence for several minutes. Finally he couldn't bear it any longer. He said in haste, "I got to go. Always remember, I love you both very much. Tell Sis I love her too. 'Bye." He hung up before he could hear their response.

A week later, Johnny was on a plane bound for Iraq. The men sat in silence, consumed with the realities of death and battle that they would soon face. Johnny was trying hard not to imagine the worst. He recalled the commitment he had made to God as a boy. It seemed to make a lot more sense now—living for eternity, serving Someone who could protect you. As he considered these things, he started to notice that, in the midst of his fear, he could sense God's presence near him for the first time in years. He asked the Lord to protect him and bring him back home alive. He promised to get serious about serving Him and thanked Him for His love. An overwhelming peace began to wash over his soul. He felt more relaxed than he had in months, and he actually fell asleep, sitting upright in the plane with his rifle in his hand.

Then he started to dream. He was standing in a thick fog, and his heart skipped a beat when someone suddenly appeared very close to him. There she was, *the woman of his dreams!* She wore a nurse's uniform again, and she seemed to be staring through him, as if she was looking for something inside of him. Somehow he knew she was searching for courage. Then she smiled, as if she had discovered it locked away in a secret chamber of his heart. Without warning, he felt boldness surge through him like a pulse of energy. She kissed him and then disappeared in the fog. He immediately woke up feeling like a different man. Boldness was still surging through him, and he was focused and confident. He knew that he would make it through whatever lay ahead. He had seen what he had to live for. The change in his attitude was so dramatic that he was convinced something supernatural had just happened to him.

The long flight came to a bumpy end when the plane touched down on a rutted dirt runway in the middle of the desert. Explosions and gunfire could be heard in the distance as the men deplaned. Within minutes, they began to sweat profusely in the 115 degree heat. "Welcome to Iraq, men," the pilot shouted. The soldiers watched the plane start to taxi down the runway. Then, to their horror, they heard an explosion of machine-gun fire. The plane burst into flames and crashed at the end of the runway in a ball of fire. The men started to run after the plane but soon had to take cover as bullets began hitting all around them. "Welcome to Iraq," Johnny repeated to himself.

It was impossible to describe the feeling of that first day in Iraq. But this was war, a man-made hell. In the months that followed, this scene repeated itself over and over again. Men died every day in battle, and Johnny struggled to cope with it. It was especially hard when the buddies he had bunked with in boot camp fell in battle. Fear, despair and hopelessness became a way of life for the men. But Johnny found that the peace and boldness that had come over him on the plane stayed with him, giving him strength and resolve that he otherwise couldn't have had in the circumstances.

Then the day came for Johnny that every solider dreads. He and his troop found themselves pinned down in an abandoned section of the city of Khafji, located on the border between Saudi Arabia and Kuwait, surrounded on three sides by the enemy. They radioed for help but were informed it would be three hours before reinforcements would arrive. Their only hope for survival was to make it to an abandoned building three hundred yards north of them and wait for help. The men had to crawl on their bellies for a couple hundred yards, then jump to their feet and sprint to the ruins amidst a hail of gunfire. When it was Johnny's turn to go, he said a quick prayer, sprang to his feet, and took off running for his life. He had almost reached a crumbling wall of the building when his helmet was struck by a piece of shrapnel and knocked from his head. He stooped down to grab it, but bullets were flying and grenades were exploding all around him, and the men were shouting and waving for him to hurry. He ducked down, rushed forward and made a final leap for the building. The men helped to drag him to safety.

Gasping for breath, he burst out, "My ring . . . my ring! I have to get my helmet!" He saw the sergeant. "Sir, I have to get my helmet!"

"Take cover, Johnson!" the sergeant shouted back.

"Sarge, you don't understand, I have to get my helmet . . . I have to go, sir!" Johnny argued wildly.

"Get down, Johnny! Do you hear me, son? Keep your head down!" the sergeant insisted.

But Johnny doggedly shook his head. "Sorry, sir. I have to get my helmet." He jumped over the barricade and ran down the littered city street with bullets whistling past his head. Seeing his helmet, he dove for it, strapped it to his head, jumped up, and rushed back. As he lunged for the barricade, bullets pierced his right thigh and knee. He screamed in pain as he struggled to crawl the last few feet to the crumbling building. Two soldiers crawled out and dragged him to safety. One of the bullets had hit an artery and he was quickly losing a lot of blood. The men ripped open his fatigues and made a tourniquet out of his belt to slow the bleeding. He heard them calling for a helicopter to take him to the MASH unit as he slipped into unconsciousness.

The chopper finally arrived at dusk and was taking fire as it attempted to land in a nearby landing zone. The men rushed Johnny to it and loaded him inside as the gunner laid cover with a 50mm machine gun. They flew Johnny to Baghdad, where he immediately went into surgery to stop the bleeding and remove the bullets. After surgery, he lay unconscious for three days, hanging on to life by a thread. But on the third morning, he finally came to. He managed to open his eyes and force himself upright, groaning. "Where am I? What's going on? What happened to me?"

"You are in the hospital," said a calm voice near his bed. "You were wounded in battle. You are going to be fine."

"My helmet . . . my helmet! Where's my helmet? I want my helmet . . . please. Please find my helmet," Johnny begged.

"Your helmet is right here." The nurse laid it on the bed next to him. Johnny reached out and grabbed it, feeling for the ring. He sighed with relief when he discovered it was still under the liner.

"Your sergeant said you were shot while retrieving it from the battlefield," the nurse said from behind him. "He wanted to make sure you had it when you woke up."

Johnny turned his head to find the source of her voice.

"I am right here," she said, grasping his head gently with both her hands and turning it until his eyes met hers. They were beautiful and green and looked into his with a steady gaze that was all too familiar. He struggled to clear his head from the fog. It was *déjà vu*. He knew this woman. Somehow, somewhere, he had met her. He recognized her voice, her eyes, her smile—but how was it possible?

Her black hair shimmered under the bright exam lights as she moved to his bedside to check his blood pressure. Her movements were elegant and graceful. Then he noticed her uniform, and the truth came over him. It was her, destiny's child, *the woman of his dreams!* He could hardly take her in. The strain and trauma of the battlefield faded from his mind and body as he became entirely transfixed by her presence. He couldn't take his eyes off of her, and it was obvious. She giggled as she tried to concentrate on taking his vitals.

"It's rude to stare at people, you know," she said.

"I can't help it."

"Hmm. I guess I shouldn't expect much from someone who's been wounded and delirious for three days."

"I may be wounded, but I am not dead," he fired back.

She smiled. "I can see that. Well, I am going to get the doctor and tell him you woke up." She started to walk away.

"Wait! Before you leave me, I have a question for you."

"What is it, Private Johnson first class?"

Summoning his courage he asked, "Will you marry me? I am serious. Will you be my wife?"

She stared at him for a moment, which seemed to him an eternity, then shook her head, turned, and walked away, laughing.

"I'm serious!" he shouted after her. He wanted to call her name, but realized he didn't know it.

Ten minutes later, the doctor walked into the room to examine him. "Good morning, Private Johnson. Maria has informed me that you are very much awake and already regaining your strength," the doctor said with a smile.

Johnny wanted to hug the doctor for saying her name. *Maria. What a beautiful name.* Johnny proceeded to think of nothing else all through his examination with the doctor. After the doctor left, however, the audacity of his impulsive proposal struck him, and he began to grow anxious that he had scared her away, as the next hour passed and Maria failed to return. But finally she appeared. He was grateful beyond belief when she came in, smiling, to tend to him. He resolved to try and be more respectful and patient in wooing her. Thankfully, since she had been assigned as his nurse, he had plenty of opportunity to prove the sincerity of his intentions.

Johnny's recovery ended up lasting several weeks. Gradually he was able to walk, assisted by Maria, and by the time he didn't need her help anymore, they had begun taking daily walks together when she got off work. It was on these walks that they had a chance to learn about each other. She told him that she was the youngest daughter of a wealthy Texas oilman and that she had decided to become a nurse against her father's wishes because she wanted to help people. She was strong and compassionate, funny and frank, and the more Johnny came to know her, the more he realized that she was more amazing than he had ever dreamed. Thankfully, she seemed to feel the same way about him, and their love grew deeper each day. But in all their conversations, he never mentioned the ring. He still planned, as he had been planning since he was 15, to surprise her with it on their wedding night.

Seven weeks after Johnny had arrived at the hospital in the Medivac helicopter, the doctor told him that he was well enough to return to light duty and that he would finish his tour back in the States. The night before his departure, Maria came into his room and knelt beside him. With tears running down her cheeks, she took his hand and said, "I would love to be your wife, Johnny." He took her in his arms and wept with her in joy and sadness. After a while, they walked out on to the back porch of the hospital and sat there in silent communion, watching the beautiful sunrise together. A few hours later, Johnny was on his way home.

The remaining months of Johnny's tour of duty seemed painstakingly long. But in spite of the oceans and thousands of miles between them, Johnny and Maria's love grew stronger. They wrote each other every day right up until the day of their wedding, which took place at Maria's family home, a lavish mansion on the Gulf of Mexico, a few days after Johnny was released from duty. The wedding was awesome—Maria's parents spent a small fortune on the celebration and invited hundreds of guests. Johnny gave Maria a simple wedding band during the ceremony, but as he did so, all he could think about was the moment when he would present her with the ring. It was all he could think about all day. It seemed like forever before they finally ran to the limo, showered in rice, and were swept away to their hotel on the beach.

They savored their first moments of the day alone together, in the back of the limo, tenderly holding hands and beholding each other in wonder. He couldn't wait to see her face when he opened the velvet box and gave her the ring—*the ring for the woman of his dreams*. It was going to be amazing.

When they got to the hotel, he picked her up and carried her to the wedding suite. Playfully he tossed her on the king-sized bed and fell on top of her as they laughed. It was all new and so exciting. Johnny had to confess to her that he was a little nervous. Maria agreed. She convinced him to let her change and retreated to the dressing room.

It was the perfect moment, so Johnny rushed to his suitcase and pulled out the ring. He hid it behind him, and grinning, shouted, "Hurry up! I can't wait any longer!"

"Good things are worth waiting for, Johnny Johnson," she said. Finally she stood before him, framed by the dressing room door. He couldn't have agreed with her more.

As she walked up to him, he said, "I have a surprise for you. Sit on the bed and close your eyes." She gave him a questioning look, but closed her eyes and sat down. "Okay, open your eyes," Johnny said, choking back tears. He was kneeling in front of her with the blue velvet box opened in his hand.

Maria smiled, but she didn't look as surprised as he had envisioned. "Oh Johnny, it's so nice. You didn't have to do that."

"Do you like it?"

"I do like it. It's lovely. Thank you so much." She put the ring on and held it up to show him. Then she knelt down beside him, put her arms around him and kissed him. "But I love you more."

As they embraced, Johnny tried to ignore the knot of disappointment in his stomach. He had hoped that the moment he'd been anticipating for five years would be a little more momentous. He looked at his beautiful bride and smiled. *So what?* he told himself. *You didn't get the moment, but you still have the woman of your dreams. Get over it.*

The next morning, they woke early and grinned at each other across the pillows. But a pang of heartache intruded into Johnny's bliss when he remembered the ring. "Are you sure you like the ring?" he asked again.

"Of course I like it, silly." She kissed him. "And I bet I can beat you to the beach." She jumped out of bed, threw on her bathing suit, and ran toward the water.

Johnny was close behind, shouting, "You better take off the ring before you get in the water!"

"It'll be fine!" she shouted back.

Soon they were in the water, frolicking wildly, splashing each other and laughing hilariously. But when they finally came back to the beach, the ring was gone!

Johnny stared at Maria's bare hand in shock. He suddenly burst into tears and staggered toward the water, sobbing. He couldn't believe it was gone. It seemed unfathomable that the thing he had worked so long for and even been shot for was lost forever. He fell to the sand in utter confusion. "It's gone . . . it's gone forever," he repeated.

Distressed, Maria knelt down next to him and wrapped her arms around him. "I'm sorry, Johnny. Please, don't be mad at me! We can buy another ring! My folks will give me the money. We'll find one just like the one you bought me. It'll be okay. Please don't cry."

But nothing she said brought him comfort. He was devastated. He had spent so much of his life working for and protecting this ring so he could present it to *the woman of his dreams*. But in the end, it meant little more to her than a commodity that could easily be replaced. How could he get her to understand that the true value of the ring was in the blood, sweat, and tears that it took to get it from the battlefield all the way to the bedroom?

CONSIDER THIS

1. What do you value the most?

   _____

   _____

   _____

   _____

   _____

   _____

   _____

   _____

   _____

   _____

   _____

   _____

2. What do you value about yourself? What qualities do you feel are vital for a husband or wife to have?

   _____

   _____

   _____

   _____

   _____

   _____

   _____

   _____

   _____

   _____

   _____

   _____

   _____

   _____

   _____

3. What value do you place on the purity of your relationship with your future husband or wife?

    _____

    _____

    _____

    _____

    _____

    _____

    _____

    _____

    _____

    _____

    _____

4. What are you willing to sacrifice to protect what you most treasure? (Consider your time, money, current relationships, lifestyle and so on.)

    _____

    _____

    _____

    _____

    _____

    _____

    _____

    _____

    _____

    _____

    _____

    _____

    _____

    _____

2

FROM THE BATTLEFIELD TO THE BEDROOM

They sat on the beach, the ocean breeze blowing through their hair, as Maria continued to try to comfort Johnny. Finally, a little frustrated, she said, "Johnny, please help me understand why you are so upset over a silly ring!"

Through his tears, Johnny began to recount the story of the ring to Maria. He described how he had worked relentlessly, forsaking everything else to earn enough money to buy the ring. He shared his Army experiences of protecting the ring and going back to rescue it from the battlefield. He told Maria of his excitement on their honeymoon night in giving her something that carried such a huge price. And then he looked into her deep green eyes and said, "You will always be the woman of my dreams! Maria, it was you I was really fighting for anyway. The ring was just a symbol of my love for you. I am sorry I got so upset over it. I guess I just got caught up in the symbol and forgot about the real reason I worked so hard to protect it."

Maria sat there for a moment, overwhelmed. It was a lot to take in—the idea that this ring, in such a strange way, had brought them together, and that the man she had married had done so much for so long to bring it to her. It felt as though she were seeing him as he truly was for the first time. Maria suddenly caught a glimpse of the true price of the ring, and she was overcome by emotion.

"Johnny," she struggled to continue. "I love you with all my heart! I never understood the value of the ring. Can you ever forgive me? I was so stupid," Maria said, now crying uncontrollably.

He embraced her, and rolling onto his back, he lifted her up on top of him. "I forgive you Maria! I really do!"

As he turned his head to kiss her, he saw something wash up on the seashore out of the corner of his eye. It was glistening on the wet sand about 20 feet from them.

"Maria! Maria, look!" Johnny shouted.

They jumped to their feet and rushed to the site. There it was, barely sticking out of the sand, *the ring for the woman of his dreams!* He reached down, picked it up, and blew the sand off of it.

Johnny began to recite, "With this ring, thee I do wed, my beloved Maria, for better or worse, for richer or poorer."

They both laughed like little children as he slipped the ring onto her finger.

Maria took Johnny's face in her hands and said, "Johnny, thank God for second chances!"

THE COST OF LOVE

Maria was raised like many kids. Her folks gave her everything she wanted when she was growing up, so she was robbed of the awesome experience of what it is like to fight or work for something precious, prized, or powerful. It took her awhile to wrap her brain around the fact that the ring wasn't just a cool piece of jewelry but that it was a sign of Johnny's love for her. When Johnny was working his butt off, he wasn't actually slaving away for a rock, but he was working for the honor of giving her a piece of his heart. His gift couldn't be replaced with money because it was never really purchased with riches. Of course, he paid for the ring with dollars, but each greenback was legal tender of his acts of sacrifice, passion, and pain. When Johnny returned to the battlefield, it wasn't to save his investment, it was to rescue his bride!

Are you getting this? Do you understand that with every act of courage, with every hour of labor, with every ounce of blood spilled, the value of the ring increased? *Anyone can give away something expensive, but only those who understand sacrifice can give away something valuable.*

But it is not just those who grow up in wealthy families who struggle to understand the high value of love. The whole world seems to have lost sight of the priceless worth of true love that flows from pure hearts and innocent souls.

UNLOCKING THE MYSTERY OF THE RING

The story you just read is an allegory, a parable if you will. Johnny is every father's son, and Maria is every mother's daughter. The ring is a symbol of your virginity, and the battle is real! *Your virginity is a treasure hidden in the vault of your life, protected by the helmet of your virtues, values and principles.* Purity is like the ring in the parable because it is a manifestation of something deeper, something worth much more than its intrinsic beauty. Much like the ring, virginity itself is beautiful, but it doesn't hold a candle to the stunning, pristine waters of the pure heart that virginity flows from.

THE BATTLEFIELD

As with any fortune, there is always a real fight to keep it in the hands of its rightful owner. In fact, this treasure is actually valued according to the warfare it takes to get it from the battlefield to the honeymoon suite. The greater the battle, the more meaningful your purity is when you finally lie with your lover. This is the reason you have a sex drive before you should have sex—so that you give your lover something you had to fight to keep. But the war isn't over on your honeymoon night! No way! The strategy changes, but the battle remains as you fight to keep your affections unpolluted and unspoiled for the woman or man of your dreams in the midst of the cesspool of a dark world that has exchanged love for lust.

But the great news is that whether you are married or single, the struggle to keep yourself pure has a divine purpose. There is an ancient story of an old, wealthy king named David that illustrates my point. This king screwed up and got in trouble with his God. A prophet named Gad came to his house and told him that, if he wanted to patch up his relationship with God, he needed to build an altar on the property of a guy named Araunah. So the king went over to the guy's house and told him he wanted to buy his property so that he could dedicate the land to his God and build an altar on it. Araunah was a generous, rich guy and he told King David he could have the property for free. This is where the story gets deep. David made a stunning statement to Araunah. He said, in essence, "I will buy it from you for the full price because I will never offer to God something that cost me nothing" (see 2 Samuel 24:18-24). Like Johnny, the king understood that he needed to give his God a piece of his soul and, therefore, that it would have to cost him something. The property became a metaphor, a love letter, an outward sign of inward passion. *You see, true love germinates in the soil of sacrifice, sprouts in the garden of surrender and matures in a matrimony of servanthood. Love isn't love until it has cost you something to give it away.*

WINNING TROPHIES

This whole idea of paying a price that is not measured in dollars makes me think of trophies. We give trophies to people for all kinds of things in our culture—spelling bees, wrestling contests, humanitarian efforts and achievements in film and music. But these trophies, like the ring and Araunah's property, are only meaningful because they represent the high cost of sacrifice. Thus, the significant thing about these trophies is not the trophies themselves, but the stories they represent—the stories of victory, hard work, excellence, creativity and sacrifice. Without the stories, they're just hunks of metal, plastic, paint or ribbon.

This point came to light a few months ago. It was Sunday morning. My seven-year-old grandson, Elijah, ran into the room carrying a trophy over his head, shouting, "Papa, Papa, look what I won! Look what I won!" He had just finished his first soccer season and, with it, gained his first taste of victory.

I looked down at the little plastic trophy and said, "Elijah, you are so amazing! I am so proud of you."

He was beaming. "I know it," he said proudly.

The trophy couldn't have cost more than a couple of dollars, but trophies are never valued in dollars. Have you ever heard of anyone at an NBA championship, the World Series or a Super Bowl celebration talking about the price of the trophy? No way, because the value of a trophy is not measured in dollars! No athlete is competing for the cost of the trophy because *it is not the trophy that gives the game value but it is the game that determines the value of the trophy*.

But as we all know, some games are simply more meaningful and some trophies more valuable than others because of the high price that the players paid to win them. For example, one of the most valuable trophies in sports history is the 1997 NBA championship trophy. On

June 11, the Chicago Bulls played the Utah Jazz in the fifth game of the playoffs. The Bulls were losing and there were only 48 seconds left on the clock. To make matters worse, the Bulls' superstar, Michael Jordan, was playing sick. He had a severe case of the flu and he kept going to the sidelines to throw up. At each timeout, doctors filled Jordon intravenously with fluids. But in spite of the circumstances stacked against him, Jordan battled back, scoring 38 points and stealing the game from the Utah Jazz in the final seconds. Throughout the entire last quarter of the game, the whole crowd, including many of the Jazz fans, was on its feet screaming and rooting for Jordan. The Bulls went on to win the championship in six games.

Another highly valued trophy is the gold medal of the 1980 Olympic hockey championship. The Americans had not won a gold medal in Olympic hockey in years. The experienced Russian team was highly favored over the young American team. But against all odds, the Americans fought their way into the playoff game against the Russians, and when the game was over, the Americans had won. The United States' team went on to beat Finland for the gold medal. The world was stunned and Americans everywhere celebrated. Most Americans had never even watched a hockey game before. But this was different—this wasn't about hockey; this was about people beating the odds, overcoming a more powerful opponent, doing the unexpected and capturing the prize.

I said a moment ago that the game determines the value of the trophy. We know that, because of the nature of professional basketball or hockey, it's a significant feat of physical training and teamwork for anyone to win in the NBA finals or the Olympics. In these particular games, these men made those feats even greater by paying a higher price than many of their colleagues. But imagine what would happen to my grandson, Michael Jordan, and all those trophies if someone managed to convince us that soccer, basketball and hockey were pointless, uninspiring games on par with pie-eating contests and pick-up-sticks? Michael, the United States' hockey team and my grandson would be playing some other game, and the trophies would be gathering dust in some basement.

Sadly, we live in a culture that no longer prizes sexual purity. The challenge called "keeping your virginity" or "saving sex for marriage" has fallen out of style, and the thought of undertaking such a challenge strikes many people as absurd and even unhealthy. Others of us have grown up in rule-keeping, religious environments and have heard the "keep your virginity" stuff for years but without a really good explanation for *why*. We're trying to play the game, but we aren't being set up to win because no one is telling us that there's a trophy worth paying a price for.

LOSERS

If you have been trying to treasure your virginity and live a pure life, you've probably found out that this is a lot more like a battle than a game. For most of us, keeping our purity is not merely a matter of exercising self-control over our sex drives. The world we live in is a minefield just daring us to try and scale the hill of holiness. We are surrounded on all sides by aggressive messages designed to get us to confuse love for lust, and we're surrounded by a bunch of people who have bought into these lies. As a result, most of these deceived people don't understand that they're in a war at all. They are ignorant lambs in a land of ravenous wolves, devoured without so much as a struggle. They succumb to peer pressure and the power of their sex drives, sleep with anyone, lose their self-respect and wonder why no one admires them. When they finally find someone special, they have nothing of value to give to them because they are all used up. Their trophy has been smashed to bits, their prize pulverized and their purity dragged through the streets of peer pressure and poverty. Their crown is lost, trampled by the crowd, and tarnished by a guilt that lingers long after their lovers leave, taking with them another piece of their heart.

Of course, most of these people embrace this version of sexuality because they are looking for love and romance. But it is driven by lust, not love, and so instead of satisfying their hearts, it leaves them twisted and even more starved than before. Thus, the search that, for so many, began as an exciting adventure ends in lonely nights and painful days. Regret eventually gives way to denial and a cycle of drowning the pain begins. In their effort to deny the damage that has been done in their lives through casual sex, most people must not only keep telling themselves that they're okay, but they must also put down anyone who's doing it right. This is why the world sneers at those who are "saving themselves" for marriage. They can't stand the idea that some people are holding on to the trophy when theirs are long gone.

After all, the only people in the world who don't like trophies are people who are playing with a losing hand. To someone who is unable to win, a trophy is a sign that they lost the race, fell short of the goal or gave up too soon in the battle. Losers like to pretend they don't care about trophies. They like to make fun of people who play to win or fight for the prize, and they give winners demeaning names like "jocks," "nerds," "front-runners," or "kiss-butts." But the real issue is that losers just don't have the guts to compete, and every time someone else wins, they are reminded again that they lost. Therefore, losers work hard to drag other people down so that they don't have to feel bad about themselves. Misery loves company! *Winners play on teams but losers hide in crowds.* Crowds seldom contain winners because winners always intimidate crowds. Crowds often sabotage their relationship with winners so that they don't have to endure great people with high standards in their face reminding them of their miserable lives of denial.

DAVID AND GOLIATH

The famous story of David and Goliath reminds me of the purity challenge. David, 15 years old and the eighth kid in his family, was ordered by his dad to bring lunch down to the battlefield for his older brothers. His brothers were among the Israelite army that had been hiding from Goliath for 39 days. David arrived just in time to hear Goliath stand up, cuss out the Israelite army and challenge them to a fight. So David asked the guy next to him who the overgrown, foul-mouthed, arrogant bozo was and what the reward was for shutting him up. When Eliab, David's oldest brother, over-heard him asking about kicking the big guy's butt, he told him to go home and play with his sheep. Nobody wants their kid brother killing a giant that they have been running from for 39 days. Sometimes before you can beat the Goliaths of your life you have to take on your brothers (see 1 Samuel 17:1-58).

This is especially true of those who have subdued their giant sex drive and made passion their slave instead of their master. Very few people who have lost their purity in the battle of "Bunk-with-her" Hill want to hang around virgins who are displaying their badge of courage.

RAGS TO RICHES

We all love "rags to riches" stories—the poor girl who made it big or the underdog who defeated the great champion. We admire people like Cinderella, who overcame her wicked stepmother, or Esther, the slave girl who became a beautiful princess and altered the course of history in a foreign land. But we often forget that these people were actually born losers and that they could have stayed that way. Cinderella could have turned into a bitter spinster, hunched over after years of hard labor. And Esther's fear could have led to an unimaginable holocaust that included her own demise. But they became winners by refusing to let their circumstances, their failures or the actions of others become their lot in life, pressing on instead to the high call of true love, humility, sacrifice and heroism. Do not let your past dictate your future. God is always there whenever you are ready to become a winner. *There is no circumstance that He can't change, no hand dealt to you with which He can't win, and no mistake so bad or sin so great that He can't fully restore you!*

The famous apostle Paul knew what it was like to be a loser. Much like the Nazis of Germany, he murdered people in the name of his religion, dragging them into the streets and stoning them while their families looked on. Seething with hatred and anger, he hunted people down like wild animals, terrorized innocent women and left thousands of children fatherless. But then one day he saw the light. His life turned around overnight, and he suddenly became a winner. In the middle of one of his life's worst battles, he wrote these encouraging words, "We are afflicted in every way, but not crushed; perplexed, but not despairing; persecuted, but not forsaken; struck down, but not destroyed" (2 Corinthians 4:8-9).

If you have failed in the battle for purity, don't get discouraged. Turn to the last chapter of this book and read Grace's story.

JILL'S STORY

I went to high school in the early '70s in the midst of the so-called Sexual Revolution. The motto of our times was, "If you can't be with the one you love, love the one you're with."[1] Of course, this song had nothing to do with love. It really meant, "Screw whoever you can; don't be loyal to anyone." There were a couple thousand kids in our high school, but I think you could count the number of virgins on two hands.

Jill Jones (not her real name) was the most popular girl in school. She was beautiful, with long blond hair, blue eyes and a great body. She was always the best-dressed woman on campus. Our school was very ethnically diverse, and prejudice was rampant, but Jill's favor somehow transcended racial tension. Everyone liked and respected her. But the most amazing thing about Jill was that she was a virgin, and everybody knew it! She carried herself like nobility, like a princess, like someone special. I loved her like a sister and looked up to her.

Then one day I was in the locker room getting dressed after P.E., and I overheard two guys talking. One guy said, "Last night I took Jill Jones to a party. I got her drunk, and I screwed her!" (As you can imagine, it was quite a bit more graphic than that.)

The other guy said, "Wow, what a score!"

I was stunned. I didn't know what to think or say. I ran all the way home, threw myself on my bed and wept for hours. I wasn't sure why I was crying, but my heart was broken, and my grief left me speechless. Looking back now, I understand that Jill was our hope. She was a lighthouse in the midst of a bad storm, a monument to the impossible. She was the underdog in the battle for righteousness, and secretly, many of us who were still virgins or wanting our purity restored were rooting for her to win.

But things got worse. Within a couple months, Jill began to dress like a slob. Her once vibrant countenance was now etched with sadness and grief. Her confidence fell away, replaced by a head hung in shame and covered by ragged, unkempt hair. Soon she was smoking and hanging out with the drug crowd. She had lost her self-respect and dropped her trophy. Instead of picking it up again, she stepped on it and smashed it into little pieces.

I saw Jill at my 30-year class reunion. She was in her third marriage and had been dragged through the mire of life, crushed by mean men, virtueless tramps. But thankfully, I learned that her story didn't end there. Later in life, Jill found the Lord. He gave her the strength and the fortitude she needed to emerge from the mire of a miserable existence. He dusted her off, recovered her purity and restored her trophy. She was older now, her beauty tempered by the sands of time. But her self-respect was back, her stately walk had returned and nobility reigned in her eyes again. I will never forget Jill. To me she is more than a fond memory. She is a lesson in life, a parable of riches to rags and rags to riches. She will forever stand as a monument in my memory—as a monument to the destruction caused by lust and shame, but far more, as a testimony to the greater power of true love and grace.

CONSIDER THIS

1. What value does the culture place on virginity? What value do you place on your sexual purity?

   _____

   _____

   _____

   _____

   _____

   _____

   _____

   _____

   _____

   _____

   _____

2. What struggles are you facing to protect your virginity—physically, emotionally, mentally? Are you willing to pay this price?

   _____

   _____

   _____

   _____

   _____

   _____

   _____

   _____

   _____

   _____

   _____

   _____

   _____

3. What satisfaction comes from fighting for something
   you treasure? What is the cost of losing the battle for
   your sexual purity?

   _____

   _____

   _____

   _____

   _____

   _____

   _____

   _____

   _____

4. How would you respond to someone who challenges
   your decision to be sexually pure? (This applies to
   those who are reclaiming their purity as well.)

   _____

   _____

   _____

   _____

   _____

   _____

   _____

   _____

   _____

   _____

   _____

   _____

Note

1. Crosby, Stills, Nash, and Young, "Love the One You're With" (lyrics and music by Stephen Stills), *4 Way Street [Live]* (Atlantic/Wea Records, 1971, 1992).

3

THE GREAT ESCAPE

It was 1969, the height of the Sexual Revolution, and I was a freshman in high school in the Bay Area of San Francisco. One of the most popular girls in school sat next to me in algebra class. Little did I know that I would actually end up flunking my algebra class because of her.

Mary (not her real name) was the head JV cheerleader. She had long brown hair, blue eyes and a great figure. I couldn't keep my eyes off of her. My mind would go completely blank whenever she was near me. I was so taken by her that every night I would lie in bed imagining what it would be like to ask her out. Several months passed, and I finally got the courage to walk with her to class. She seemed so amazing. As the months passed, I gained more confidence and finally asked her to be my girlfriend. She said yes! I couldn't believe that I was dating one of the most popular girls on campus.

One day I told Mary I would walk her home, which I then learned was two miles from our high school, in the opposite direction of my house. When the last bell rang that day, I ran to her class to greet her. I was so excited to be with her. When she emerged from the classroom, she offered me her hand. I took it, and we began the long walk to her house. I felt like "The Man" as we walked down the busy street hand in hand. As we neared her home, time seemed to stand still.

"My parents aren't home today," Mary said with a silly grin.

I couldn't figure out why she was telling me about her parents' schedule. I was so intoxicated with her that her comments went right over my head. We finally arrived at her driveway.

"My parents just bought a new waterbed," she said, breaking the silence again.

Now she is telling me about their furniture, I thought. It made no sense to me. Was she just trying to make small talk, or was there something significant about her parents' furniture? I just didn't get it.

I walked her to the front door of her house, and we stood on the porch staring into each other's eyes. As I leaned over to kiss her good-bye, she said in a seductive tone, "Would you like to come in and try out my parents' new waterbed?"

Her words hit me like a ton of bricks. I was stunned! I just stood there staring at her. I tried to form words, but my mouth wouldn't cooperate. I didn't know what to think. It wasn't as though I didn't want her—oh boy, I wanted her so badly. But there was something in me that didn't want it to be like this. My mind was flooded with thoughts that seemed to come at me from a hundred different directions, and my soul was overwhelmed with emotion. My heart was pounding out of my chest. Part of me was saying, *One of the most popular girls in the world just invited you to have sex with her. Dude, you are about to become one of the most popular guys in school. You are finally getting off of the porch of purity and running with the big dogs!* But another part of my brain was yelling, *Get out of here while you still can! You have been saving yourself all these years. Don't let this woman destroy your values!*

The war inside of me was intense. I stood there for what seemed like an eternity. Then, without warning, I took off running. I ran the entire four miles home without stopping. I was so embarrassed and confused. I could hardly sleep all night, wondering what she was thinking of me, and more importantly, what she was going to tell all of our classmates. I kept imagining a banner over the school lawn that read, "KRIS VALLOTTON IS A NERD." The next morning, I couldn't find the courage to go to school, so I faked being sick the rest of the week and stayed home. When I did return to school, I cut my algebra class for the rest of the year so that I wouldn't have to face Mary.

Thankfully, in the three years following this incident that we went to school together, she never brought it up to me once. There was never a single rumor about it flying around school, and our mutual friends didn't ever talk to me about it. Looking back, I think Mary was more concerned about me exposing her than I was about being called a nerd.

But five years later, on my honeymoon night in Santa Cruz, California, in a hotel room overlooking the beach, I had a completely different perspective. That night I didn't feel like a nerd at all. Actually, I felt like a champion. I had resisted Mary, braved the social elements and managed to escape a pit of destruction. To this day, I don't really know if it was divine intervention, my desire to stay pure or the raw fear of failure that sent me running, but whatever it was, I can say now with all honesty and gratitude that I have had sex with only one woman in my entire life—the woman of my dreams, my wife of 35 years, Kathy.

LIVING WITH PURPOSE

While I may have escaped the trap of promiscuity in high school, however, I am all too aware that the Sexual

Revolution has taken its toll and shifted the sexual morals of our culture. Most everyone growing up in our society today is being presented with far more opportunities to be promiscuous than I was, and our educational system is passionately intent on numbing our conscience and even stripping away the natural convictions that we grow up with about sex. For that reason, I believe that young people today need more in their arsenal when it comes to navigating this sexual culture than I had. In short, they need a vision.

There is an ancient Hebrew proverb that says, "Where there is no vision, the people are unrestrained [or perish], but happy is he who keeps the law" (Proverbs 29:18). *THE MESSAGE* Bible reads, "If people can't see what God is doing, they stumble all over themselves; but when they attend to what He reveals, they are most blessed." You might ask, "What does that have to do with purity?" Great question. When the Bible is talking about the law here, it is not referring merely to the Ten Commandments. It is speaking more generally about the law of restraint. In other words, when we have a vision for our lives, we restrain our options to capture the vision. But if we have no vision, we perish or stumble because we end up spending all of our energy either trying to find pleasure or working to stay out of pain.

Maybe it would be helpful if I gave you an example. Let's say I get tired of being overweight and decide that I want to have a great body. So I go down to the local gym and work out for a couple of hours. But the next morning, I wake up feeling like I have been run over by a Mack truck. There is only one thing that is going to get me back to the gym day after day, and that one thing is a *vision* for an awesome body. But without a vision, I will continue to sabotage my health by giving in to my body's desire for comfort. *Vision gives pain a purpose!* It's vision that causes me to restrain my eating, rework my calendar and reprioritize my life to capture the dream of having a great body. I will never build a great body by not wanting to be fat. It is vision that gives me the strength to reorder my life so that I can achieve my goals.

One of the greatest decisions we have to make concerning vision is how we *envision* ourselves. Therefore, the billion-dollar question is: Who do you think you are? Our behavior flows from the vision that we have for ourselves. Once we decide *who* we are, then we will naturally work out our actions, attitudes and behaviors to manifest our person. But if we don't settle this question in our hearts, then two things most often occur. First we begin to look to other people to tell us who we are. This leads to us becoming whatever others need us to be to fulfill their imagination. Soon we find ourselves in the very dangerous place of developing intimate relationships with people so that we can draw strength and self-esteem from them. I don't mean that other people can't encourage us, but if we live to fulfill someone else's vision for our lives, we transfer the responsibility for our personal choices to someone else. This begins the unhealthy pattern of behaving to please people instead of living out of the virtues that are rooted in our personal vision.

This is especially true of romantic relationships. It is vitally important that we answer the question, "Who am I?" *before* getting into a romantic relationship with someone. Otherwise, the relationship will be codependent instead of interdependent. A codependent relationship is created anytime our happiness, wellbeing or identity is predominantly dependent upon another person. When we give anybody this place in our lives, they become so powerful in the relationship that they take the place of God. This occurs most often when we lose sight of who we are and we begin to create a list of expectations for other people to fulfill so we can feel important, significant or powerful. But nobody can actually make us happy or feel significant for any length of time. Happiness is an inside job, and true significance comes as we take ownership of our own inner world.

The second thing that happens when we lack vision for ourselves is that we live without restraint. Our behavior is sold into slavery to our emotions, and our emotions become a taskmaster, dictating to us how we will behave. Our theme song becomes, "If it feels good, do it," and we rarely consider how today's behavior is affecting tomorrow's destiny, not to mention the lives of those we love.

There is no middle ground in this issue of identity. Either we take responsibility to know ourselves, and we make choices that have integrity with who we are, or we surrender that responsibility to other people, our physical impulses or other circumstantial influences. When we do the latter, we cannot help but end up in bondage, controlled by forces outside of us. But when we have a vision for our lives, we become free people as we live out of our virtues in order to capture our vision. Free people can handle liberty because they have developed character through exercising the restraint dictated by their virtues. They are not the slaves of their physical desires; rather, they train their bodies to behave in order to fulfill the higher desires created by their own virtues.

The fact of the matter is that the war over your virginity is so strong that you are going to have to have a vision for your purity to win. I mean, you must decide that you want to be a virgin *before* you start searching for the man or woman of your dreams. You just can't wait until the windows of the car are steamed up to decide who you are going to be.

LIVING FROM YOUR VIRTUES

Years ago, I read a book about the life of Benjamin Franklin. The author recounted that Franklin decided who he wanted to be early in his life, and he wrote 13 virtues to guide all of his decisions so that he would become that person. Benjamin Franklin didn't want his emotions, his circumstances or the pressure of pleasing others to determine his destiny, define his personhood or dictate his legacy.[1] I was so inspired by the idea that I could live out of my virtues instead of living from the circumstances of my life that I wrote my own virtue list. The process of envisioning who I was created and called to be and then writing down the virtues that would enable me to become that person was so exciting. Here are a few of my own— maybe they will help to inspire you also:

- I will serve God first and honor Him always, both in life and in death.

- I will be honest, loyal, trustworthy and a man of my word, no matter what the price.

- I will keep my values, regardless of how much they cost me, and if I fail, I will be quick to repent.

- I will treat all people with respect, whether they are friend or foe, because they were created in God's image.

- I will strive to love everyone, despite their opinions, attitudes or persuasions and in spite of how they treat me.

- I will be loyal to my wife, both in thought and deed into eternity.

- I will live to bless and empower the generations to come and leave an inheritance both in the Spirit and in the natural for three generations.

· I will never work for money or sell myself at any price. I will only be motivated to do what I believe to be the right thing and receive my sustenance from God. I vow to be generous no matter what my circumstances may be.

· I will live my life to bring out the best in people and to bring them into an encounter with the real and living God.

Virtues help us to live from the inside out instead of from the outside in. No longer do I live by other people's rules. Instead, I live by values that guide my attitudes, which in turn determine my choices. Choices dictate my behavior. My behaviors become manifestations of my personhood, and my personhood leads me into my destiny.

SETTING BOUNDARIES

Once you decide *who* you are supposed to be, life is much simpler. All you have to do is live like you believe it. You'll know when you really believe in your own destiny when you *start treating yourself* as you have envisioned yourself.

You communicate to other people how to behave in your presence by the way you treat yourself. For example, if I go over to your house and the place is completely trashed (the lawn is a foot high, there are junk cars all over the front yard and inside the house is full of garbage), it tells me what is acceptable in your home. I may not put my feet up on my coffee table at my home, but I bet I would at yours. On the other hand, if you are a big pig and you come over to my house and the place is immaculate, the environment that I have created around me dictates how to behave when you are in my presence. In other words, for the most part, people treat you the way you

treat yourself. If you treat yourself like crap, you are inviting other people to do the same. If you carry yourself like
a prince or princess, others will relate to you like one.

I can't tell you how many people I have talked to over
the years who say things like, "No one respects me," "Nobody likes me," or, "No one wants to be my friend." What
they don't realize is that *they* don't like and respect themselves. They aren't good friends with themselves, but they
want others to be friends with them. That never works. We
tell people what to think of us, not so much with our
words but by the environment we develop around us and
by the way we take care of ourselves.

Of course, there are always a few people in the world
who are so miserable that they actually enjoy throwing
junk in other people's yards and messing up their homes,
metaphorically speaking. This is why we have to set up
boundaries in our lives that we don't allow ourselves or
others to cross. Boundaries are the rules of war and the
laws of constraint that are dictated by our virtues. We develop these in order to protect our investment in the person that we are working so hard to become.

We communicate where the survey stakes of our
boundaries are in several different ways. First of all, we
convey them by both the words we speak and the words
we are willing to listen to. Second, we share them by the
way we behave and by the way we allow others to behave in
our presence. They are especially exposed in the choices
that we make under pressure. And finally, we define our
boundaries through the people with whom we choose to
spend time and allow to influence us. The Bible says, "Bad
company corrupts good morals" (1 Corinthians 15:33). It
is true that we are known by the friendships we keep. That
doesn't mean that we can't have friends who are messed
up, but the question we have to ask ourselves is, "Who is

influencing whom?" If our friends refuse to keep our boundaries and insist on crapping in our yards, then we *must* inform them that their behavior is unacceptable. If they continue to act like idiots, then we have to decide why it would make sense for us to have relationships with people who have no respect for our values.

The truth is, some of us are so needy that we keep friends at any cost. The problem is that once we get a reputation for hanging out with people who allow themselves to be controlled by their lusts, it is hard to convince healthy people that we are worthy of their friendship. Most likely, they will reject us to save themselves from getting sucked into our circle of influence. This usually begins a pattern in our lives of hanging out with people who lack vision, boundaries, integrity and self-respect because no one else will have us. Again, if we allow people to get close to us who continually violate our values and break our boundaries, then we need to ask ourselves why we are hanging out with them. I believe that many times we just don't have the guts to look in the mirror and ask ourselves the hard, soul-searching questions that lead to real change in our lives.

FISHING FOR THE CATCH!

Where you fish for romance and the bait you use to catch a mate says a lot about the virtues you live by. If you are fishing the shark-infested waters of bars and parties, especially if you fish with bait that only sharks bite, please don't be shocked when you catch a hammerhead. The type of bait you use often determines the kind of fish you catch. Ladies, if you are trolling for men with your boobs, butt, or belly button, you are fishing for them by stimulating their sex drive. A man's sex drive is inspired predominantly through sight, unlike most women's, which is stimulated primarily through touch. If you use this kind of bait, you will probably catch a man who is not living from the virtues and values that you respect but is instead thinking with his penis.

Contrary to the popular stereotype in our culture, there are men who are pure. They have trained their bodies and minds to obey the restraints required by the virtues that they have embraced. And they are going to be attracted to the same kind of woman. When you dress provocatively, a virtuous man believes that you are primarily interested in attracting sex, not a respectful relationship. The guys that desire a lady who has values, virtues and assets beyond the bedroom will not be attracted to someone trolling for sharks. In fact, you are torturing the virtuous men around you when you dress like a Victoria's Secret mannequin. So you have to ask yourself the question, "Why am I dressing like this?" Is your inner person so empty, bare and bankrupt that you have nothing to offer a virtuous man?

IF IT'S NOT FOR SALE, DON'T ADVERTISE

It may feel great to receive admiration and attention from men when you put your body on display. But you need to know or remember that this admiration is totally superficial. It is the same kind of admiration that they have for any other beautiful *object*. If you want to be admired and respected for who you are as a person, then you need to present your physical body in a way that sends that message. When the Federal Reserve picks up the cash from banks, they don't stack it in a sports car, put the top down and drive through town showing it off. No, instead they carry it in an armored vehicle because it is so valuable. They could rush it to the vault faster in a Ferrari, but there is a much better chance of getting the bucks to the bank in a Brinks truck.

Ladies, the moral to this story is, *if it isn't for sale, don't advertise!* I don't mean that you should embrace the spirit of ugly or that you shouldn't look beautiful, dress nicely or smell like a million bucks. I am simply saying that there is a huge difference between looking pretty and being sexy. Even the Bible acknowledges women who were extraordinarily attractive. It says that Queen Esther and Jacob's wife Rachel were beautiful in "form and face" (Esther 2:7; Genesis 29:17). They had nice bodies. Not only that, the Bible also recognizes many other women who God Himself calls "beautiful." Please do not hear me telling you to get religious or to become some kind of prude. I am telling you to be conscientious about how you are presenting your body to people. Whether you mean to or not, you need to know that when you wear tight clothes, short dresses, low-cut shirts or blouses that expose your belly, it isn't sending a message that you want people to be attracted to you as a person. Rather, it tells them that you want them to see you as a sexual object.

Of course, let's be realistic here, there will always be a few fools who try to rob Brinks trucks even though they are armored, and likewise, we all know that there will always be virtue-less, horny suckers who will manage to sexualize anything that walks, no matter how she dresses. You can't really do much about that. The more you grow as a person, the less that superficial attention will hold any interest for you. You will naturally communicate to those around you that you respect them as people and that you expect them to do the same to you.

Anyone who wants a lifelong relationship should have the common sense to look around and realize that everyone on the planet is aging. Physical attraction and sex alone simply cannot be the foundation for a relationship that has any hope of longevity. It is wisdom to invest in becoming a person whose inner qualities will continue to grow stronger and more beautiful as you age. Think about it girls, do you really want to live with someone the rest of your life who married you for your body? Have you ever thought about the pressure of what it would be like to age with a "girl watcher"? What is your man going to do when a more beautiful woman comes along? Remember the way you attracted him in the first place? Pretty scary!

Ladies, real men are attracted to women who take an honest interest in them and see the treasure that lies in the depths of their hearts. The truth is that most men are pretty insecure in the presence of a true princess. They need some reassurance that you see something valuable in them and believe in them. What I have observed over the years is that the most physically attractive women are usually not the ones who get married first. More often, they are the ones who know how to make men feel special, valued and gifted—the ones who capture their hearts. It's really not that hard to make a man feel this way. Just taking a sincere interest in someone and asking the right questions to discover his true passion goes a long way toward breaking down the walls of fear and insecurity.

Sometimes, it seems like women who are pure protect themselves with walls of indifference and then wonder why men don't take an interest in them. It isn't necessary to be a cold fish or to conduct yourself in a businesslike manner to protect your trophy. You can be inviting and friendly without being sexy.

Women who use their sexuality to attract men have one of three things going on in them, in my estimation. Some of them are shallow because they have relegated the benefit of their lives to their bodies and have never cultivated any depth in the rest of their being. Others are afraid of men and have learned early in life how to control them through seduction. Many ladies who grew up with angry or unsafe fathers, abusive brothers or scary men in their lives discover the *not-so-well-kept secret* that they could charm the one-eyed snake in these men and subdue them under a seductive spell. The third reason that some women act seductively is that they have fallen in love with someone who has a screwed up value system. These women don't understand how to set boundaries, or they simply don't have the spiritual and emotional fortitude to take a stand for their virtues. In every case, you are dealing with people who are unhealthy. Unless you want their issues to become your issues, you might want to think twice about investing your time with them.

A MAN WITH A PLAN

Guys, all of the principles that I have just shared with the women apply to you also. If you allow your hormones to choose your women for you, you will be sorry in the end. A true princess is not going to be attracted to a snob, a slob or a swinger. They are looking for someone who shows them honor and respect, a man who pursues them like a valued jewel, not like a dog in heat. It is important that you make them feel safe, secure and protected.

I surveyed several single women and asked them what qualities they want most in a guy. Here are their answers in the order they listed them.

#1 INTEGRITY
I would like have a deep relationship with a man who has *integrity;* that you are who you say you are, which means you don't make promises that you cannot keep. Metaphor-

ically speaking, it is vital that you are not "writing checks" physically, emotionally and spiritually without the money in the bank to cash them.

#2 HONESTY

I need a man who is *honest*, transparent and vulnerable—first with himself, then with me. It is painful when men are dishonest and keep things in the shadows. The fruit of an honest man is that he makes me feel safe.

#3 CONFIDENCE

I love a man who is confident. *Confidence* coupled with humility is a beautiful thing, but pride sucks. I don't need you to have it all together, I just need you to trust the Lord and not live in fear so that you are able to lead our relationship well. When you pursue my heart with confidence and a plan to bring strength to the relationship, my confidence grows as well.

#4 SELF-SACRIFICE AND LOVE

I want a man who is *sacrificial* and knows how to *love* in a way that makes me feel valued. I want him to help meet my needs even when it is difficult, so that I know I am unconditionally loved throughout all of the circumstances of life.

GENERAL STATEMENTS WOMEN MADE

When a man is interested in me, I would like him to pursue me with a plan. If he is not at a place in his life where he is ready to be married, then I do not want him pursuing me. He does not necessarily have to know that he is going to marry me, he just has to have intentions of pursuing someone to marry. He cannot have the mindset of just having fun with a cool chick, and "maybe she'll end up being the one." He has to be purposeful as he pursues my heart. He cannot put me in the "friend" category, while treating me like a girlfriend. I want to know where he stands in the pursuit, so I do not misjudge and give more of myself than he is ready for or asking for. Guys need to make sure that their intimacy level matches their commitment level.

HAVING A MENTOR

Guys, being connected to a role model or mentor is imperative for success in these areas. Inviting someone into your life who you are real and raw with, someone who can crack your heart wide open in all areas is invaluable. Many men hide their weaknesses hoping that no one will ever truly see the "real" them. But hiding your flaws only allows your dysfunctional cycle to continue. It is only when you are real with God, with yourself and with others that you begin to become healthy and find freedom and wholeness in your life.

MY GIRL

When I was growing up, I had a lot of girlfriends in school. But because I struggled with really low self-esteem, I typically hung out with young women who had no self-respect or boundaries in their lives. Girls who carried themselves with honor scared the heck out of me. Consequently, my mom didn't like any of my girlfriends. She told me that I didn't understand how to find a real woman. I was clueless. I didn't know what she meant. Then in the summer of 1971, a 12-year-old girl came to my house to return something I had left at the lake where I had met her a week earlier on vacation. I invited her in the house for a few minutes and introduced her to my mother. After she left, my mother turned to me and said, "Son, now that's the marrying kind!"

"Come on, Mom," I said sarcastically, "she is 12 years old." (I was 15 at the time.)

"I don't care if she is ten. She is still the marrying kind!" she snapped back.

As the weeks went by, I began to think about the virtues that my mom was trying to communicate to me that made someone the "marrying kind." Many of the values that I shared with you in this chapter came from those talks that I had with my mother. It was Mom who first recognized the qualities of a real woman in Kathy. She pointed out to me that Kathy was unselfish, that she truly valued me and that she believed in who I was as a person. She could tell that Kathy was a healthy person, not someone who needed a boyfriend to improve her self-esteem or social class. She wasn't seductive or emotionally needy, but instead, she was confident and well-adjusted. She had self-respect, and she carried herself with a sense of nobility.

As time went on, I took my mother's advice, and five years later, I married that girl. It has been 40 years since my mom called Kathy the "marrying kind." I know now more than ever that my mother was right. We have been married for 35 years. We have traveled the world together, raised four children, owned nine businesses and have even gone broke once together. We have been pulled through knotholes, drug through the river, attacked by the alligators of life and counted as dead more than once, but we have *never* had a bad day in our relationship (we have had several bad hours over the years)! Our marriage reads like something out of a storybook for kids, and it's all because I listened to my mother and obeyed my heavenly Father. I have learned from them that the same values that it takes to attract a healthy woman are the virtues that are necessary to sustain a healthy marriage.

Healthy courting relationships create a foundation for strong marriages. You can't build a beautiful mansion on a rotten foundation. The point is this—don't get married until you have worked through your issues in your dating relationship. Some people have a messed up courtship, and they think marriage will solve their issues . . . *not!* Screwed up courtships create screwed up marriages because the heart issues are the same.

TIPS

It is my conviction that we are living in a generation that is perishing for lack of vision and that this lack of vision is connected to the fact that this generation is fatherless. From the most basic levels, we receive our identities from our parents. In particular, we receive our gender identity and our pattern of relating to the opposite sex through our parents. For this reason, I used to say something to my four teenagers when they were searching for their soul mates. I told my girls, "Watch how the young men you date treat their mothers. Because when your honeymoon is over, they will care for you in the same way they cared for their mother." And I said to my boys, "Pay attention to how your girlfriends interact with their fathers, because as soon as the wedding is over, that's how she will relate to you." I still believe that this is great advice today. Of course, there will always be some exceptions to this rule. But by and large, we learn to relate to the opposite sex through our parents.

Another important thing to look for in a life partner is self-love. Jesus said, "Love your neighbor as [you love] yourself" (Mark 12:31). In other words, the standard with which you love yourself becomes the measure with which you will love others. Paul said it this way, "Husbands ought also to love their own wives as their own bodies. He who loves his own wife loves himself; for no one ever hated his own flesh, but nourishes and cherishes it, just as Christ also does the church" (Ephesians 5:28-29). The bottom line is this; if the person you are interested in doesn't love him- or herself, he or she won't love you when the honeymoon is over! I am not talking about being self-centered. I am simply saying that the standard, the high-water mark of your love for your spouse, will be you. So learn to love yourself—because God does, and He is always right.

CONSIDER THIS

1. What situations, people and personal desires tempt you to compromise your resolve to be sexually pure? Which ones are the hardest to resist? Be specific.

_____

_____

_____

_____

_____

_____

_____

_____

_____

_____

2. How does the war for your purity distort how you see yourself? How does it mess with your convictions?

_____

_____

_____

_____

_____

_____

_____

_____

_____

_____

_____

_____

_____

_____

3. How does having a clear vision of who you are help you resist the temptation to compromise? How does it give you purpose as you fight for your purity?

_____

_____

_____

_____

_____

_____

_____

_____

_____

_____

_____

_____

4. Look closely at yourself. What about you best defines who you are? What motivates your attitudes and behaviors? What can you do to strengthen God's place in your life?

_____

_____

_____

_____

_____

_____

_____

_____

_____

_____

_____

_____

_____

Note

1. Benjamin Franklin, *The Autobiography of Benjamin Franklin*, quoted from "The Electric Ben Franklin," p. 38. http://www.ushistory.org/franklin/autobiography/page38.htm

4

RULES OF WAR:

WHAT HAPPENED
WHILE I WAS ASLEEP?

You remember what it was like. One day you were riding down Destiny Lane on your little pony, minding your own business, and then, BAM! You hit puberty. WOW! Suddenly you were knocked off that pony and thrown onto the back of a wild stallion. A whole new world appeared before your eyes, and you started feeling things that seemed completely irrational, scary and exciting all at the same time. It was all so weird and hard to understand—the attraction, the passion, the burning desire to be together and the *raging sex drive!* When our bodies start changing without our permission and we start having thoughts and desires that we'd never imagined before, it's hard enough to grasp what's going on, much less to know how we're supposed to feel about it all. Should we feel guilty or ashamed, or is this all normal?

To make matters worse, the rules of engagement seem to be contrary to all of your passions. You are told, "It is a sin before God to have sex before you are married! You will get a disease, become pregnant/get someone pregnant and ruin your life." Of course, there are always people on the other side of the tracks who are telling you the opposite: "It's okay—everybody's doing it. Have fun. Screw anybody you want. It is your body, and you can do anything you want with it. After all, why would God give you a sex drive if He didn't want you to have sex?"

Obviously, I am one of the voices encouraging you that sex belongs in marriage. At the most basic level, the choice to follow the impulses of our sex drive without certain limits has serious consequences, even if you succeed in avoiding pregnancy and STDs. More generally, as we've seen, the decision to allow any of our physical impulses to rule us is a recipe for disaster. We have to set limits for how we act on our desires if we are going to be healthy. The only way to set healthy limits is to understand the greater purpose for our lives. This is why I challenged you in the last chapter to decide *who* you want to be and then to identify and commit to virtues that manifest your personhood and guide your behavior, particularly when it comes to your sex drive. That vision isn't attainable without understanding and taking the steps that lead to it. So in this chapter, I want to talk to you about developing a plan for purity, a strategy for bridling the wild stallion in you. (Obviously, if you have decided to live a virtue-less life, you need not read this chapter.)

WINNING THE INNER BATTLE

Someone once said, "The problem with life is that it is so *daily*." I agree! Many of us have great ideas about life, about what it should be like and how we can become successful at it. But for most of us, the struggle lies in daily walking out our convictions—especially when it comes to thinking in such a way that our *minds* don't violate our *hearts*. Ultimately, true success lies in your ability to manage your inner life, the secret kingdom that lives within you. It is really impossible to control your behavior long-term unless you master your thoughts and subject them to the virtues that you have chosen to live by. In the last chapter, I stated that your virtues train your attitudes, attitudes dictate your choices, choices decide your behavior and your behavior determines your destiny. The way that this whole process begins is by giving your virtues authority over your thoughts. If your virtues do not govern what you allow yourself to think about, this process of reaching your destiny will be sabotaged. Trying to behave inside your virtues, without taking control of what movie is being shown in the theater room of your heart, simply won't work. Everything in life begins with a thought, an image that is projected on the movie screen of your mind.

Nothing has ever been invented that wasn't first assembled in the invisible realm of the intellect. Likewise, no war has ever been fought in the observable empire that wasn't initially fought in the secret place of someone's imagination. And no one has ever had sex with someone without first imagining it in the private room of his or her mind. This principle is so powerful that Jesus said that lusting after someone in your heart is the same thing as committing adultery with that person (see Matthew 5:28). Jesus insists that we live from the inside out and not from the outside in.

Your mind is the battlefield of your life. It is here that the war for your destiny is fought. Your thoughts are the weapons of warfare. In the midst of this battlefield, fortresses are constructed from the building blocks of imaginations that either protect lies and fantasies or safeguard truth. If you submit your mind to fantasies that undermine your virtues and values, soon a stronghold is built that protects these lies in the middle of the battlefield. You can always tell when the evil fortress is completed by the fact that you begin to defend your right to behave in a way that contradicts your core convictions.

But when you train your thoughts and actions to agree with your virtues and healthy core values, righteous castles are erected that defend your integrity and apprehend your divine destiny. One of the ways that integrity is created and preserved in your life is by not allowing your thoughts to violate your virtues. Integrity means that you are the same person on the inside that you are on the outside. Many years ago, the great apostle Paul put it this way:

> Be anxious for nothing, but in everything by prayer and supplication with thanksgiving let your requests be made known to God. And the peace of God, which surpasses all comprehension, will guard your hearts and your minds in Christ Jesus. Finally, brethren, whatever is true, whatever is honorable, whatever is right, whatever is pure, whatever is lovely, whatever is of good repute, if there is any excellence and if anything worthy of praise, dwell on these things. The things you have learned and received and heard and seen in me, practice these things, and the God of peace will be with you (Philippians 4:6-9).

Learning to control your thoughts, instead of allowing your thoughts to control you, is probably the single greatest secret to successful living. I once observed a scene that illustrates what happens when you are controlled by your thoughts. I saw a young, petite woman walking two huge dogs. The dogs were practically dragging her down the street, peeing on people's bushes and dumping in their yards, while she tugged on their leashes, trying to get them to stop. It so reminded me of the way that some people think. Their thoughts drag them through the streets of life, destroying the vegetation of their virtues and values because they have never subjected them to any kind of obedience training.

The reason our thoughts are so powerful is that they are always connected to our desires. Our thoughts have the power to awaken desires in us, and our desires have the power to create thoughts in our minds—a kind of intellectual ecosystem. The latter describes what is going on when you hit puberty. The desires triggered by your newly awakened sex drive start sending all sorts of thoughts through your mind that you haven't had to deal with before. If you are going to be able to keep these dogs on their leash, then you need to learn how to train them.

When the dogs of desire start to tug on your heart leash, it is essential to remember where your sex drive came from in the first place. It was God who activated the human sex drive by saying, "Be fruitful and multiply" (Genesis 1:28). (Did He do a great job of that or what?) Having a desire for sex is *normal*, not something that you should feel guilty about. As a matter of fact, the Bible says, "it is better to marry than to burn with passion" (1 Corinthians 7:9). *THE MESSAGE* Bible puts it in a kind of funny way. It translates the phrase "burn with passion" as "sexually tortured!" It's better to marry than to be sexually tortured. Wow, what a clear picture of the battle that wages inside of you.

Sadly, so many people withdraw from God in their teen years because they feel guilty for having sexual desires. They begin to believe lies about themselves, thinking, "I must not be a righteous person because of these desires. There is something wrong with me." That's just not true! Sex was God's idea, and it's *good*. The goal is not to get rid of your sex drive, but that you manage your appetites. It is important that you rule your passions, and not the other way around.

A COVENANT WITH YOUR EYES

What you watch with your eyes will largely determine if you are walking the dogs of desire or if they are walking you. Sight inspires your imagination more than any of the other five senses besides physical touch. And remember, the most powerful sex organ in your body is actually your brain. If you are regularly feeding your brain images that are designed to inspire lust, it is going to be difficult to rule your thoughts and keep from violating your virtues. Jesus said, "The eye is the lamp of the body; so then if your eye is clear, your whole body will be full of light" (Matthew 6:22). That word for "clear" is also translated "single." *Single* here means "without compromise."[1] If you are not compromising your heart by what you look at, you will bring wholeness, purity, and light into your body. But if your eyes compromise your heart, it will bring darkness into your life.

Job, one of the most righteous men in history, made a revealing statement about his plan for purity. He said, "I made a covenant with my eyes not to look with lust at a young woman" (Job 31:1, *NLT*). I would urge you to include a similar commitment in your covenant of purity before God. Obviously, if Jesus told us that looking at someone with lust is the same as committing adultery, then we have to have more in our plan than a simple goal to be virgins on our honeymoon nights. We have to have a plan for what we allow ourselves to look at, and how we look at it.

There is no question that the whole purpose of pornography is to inspire lust. Filmmakers who include scantily clad women and graphic sex scenes in their movies are hoping to profit from the same desire. We live in a culture that is constantly committing visual adultery, and we probably can't even begin to realize how much this has poisoned our ability to look at one another with pure eyes. We have all been exposed to images that we would have been better off never seeing. God doesn't hold us accountable for what comes across our path but for what captures our attention and our hearts. And He is able to restore us when we have been defrauded by the world.

MASTURBATION

Often people will ask me if masturbating oneself is an acceptable and honorable way to help control their sex drive while they are single. Before I give you my opinion, let's talk through the facts. The Bible instructs us in all aspects of sexuality. For example, it tells us that having sex outside of marriage is wrong and destructive (see Ephesians 5:3; Revelation 2:20). It makes it clear that sex with animals is an abomination (see Exodus 22:19; Deuteronomy 27:21). God tells us that sexual intercourse with a person of the same gender is a sin against yourself and against Heaven (see Leviticus 18:22; Romans 1:24-28). The list of sexual do's and don'ts in the Bible goes on and on, but it never mentions masturbation. Think about it, in more than 1,700 pages, written over several thousand years by more than 40 authors in many different countries and cultures, the Bible doesn't mention masturbation once—that's right, not one time.

So does God's silence on an issue that every generation has obviously faced mean it's okay to do it or that He doesn't care about it? No, actually it tells us that He has given us permission to work it out personally with Him within the boundaries of the virtues and values that He has already revealed to us. We know that, according to Christ, looking at someone with lust is the same is committing adultery (see Matthew 5:28). Therefore, it stands to reason that masturbating while fantasizing about someone clearly violates your integrity and corrupts your heart.

I once counseled an older gentleman who had masturbated seven times a day since he was 13. It had become such bondage that it literally took over his life. Anything that masters you is an addiction, and it will eventually destroy you. Addictions grow in the basement of denial. Denial means that you avoid the root issues that cause pain in your heart by covering them up with pleasure. That's the reason that sexual addictions are rampant in our world.

Many people have a monster in their basement, and they try to pretend he isn't really there. They just turn the stereo up so that they can't hear him breathing through the keyhole. And every once in a while, they throw him a steak or two to try to calm him down so the neighbors won't find out he is imprisoned down there. But as each day passes, the monster grows stronger, until finally one day he tears the basement door off its hinges and murders everyone in the house. Masturbation is the ultimate stereo, covering up the growling noises in the basement of our hearts. If we deny the root cause for an overactive sex drive, it will eventually destroy us.

One of the biggest misconceptions about masturbation is the thought that, "Someday when I get married it will all go away." This type of thinking, although it seems logical, is usually a setup for disaster. Oftentimes men use masturbation as a way to release tension or pressure, or even to curve the sting of rejection. Typically, these types of habits are carried into the marriage and not left in singlehood. The problem with this is that you begin to steal from your partner what is rightfully hers. Allow me to explain. In a marriage, a man's sex drive should motivate him to do things that he wouldn't normally do in order to connect to his wife. So a man who is feeling horny is going to do the dishes, clean the kitchen, connect to his wife emotionally and probably even watch a chick-flick because he has the need to be intimate with his wife. That same man, if he took care of his own need and just went in the bathroom and masturbated, would lose all the drive to pursue her and go the extra mile because he took care of his need on his own. In the same way, women who get their emotional needs met from soap operas, romantic films and the like rob themselves of the motivation to pursue their husbands. Therefore, the marriage suffers.

Okay, so what is the moral of the story? If you are going to masturbate to curb your sexual appetite, make sure it doesn't violate your relationship with Heaven, and be certain that you are not using it to avoid deeper issues in your life. If you do it often, you are covering up deeper issues in your heart. Don't ever let your appetites control you; you must manage them. And don't sexualize people to satisfy your sex drive. Keep your heart pure in all that you do.

COVENANT CONNECTION

Because God is the One who designed and activated your sex drive, it follows that He has both wisdom and strength for directing it toward its true purpose. He doesn't want you to withdraw from Him as you deal with your thoughts and feelings; He wants you to run to Him. The foundations of the castle walls that protect your virtues and values are poured in the concrete of a covenant connection with God. The war in your soul can get so intense, at times, that you will need His help to win these battles and hold on to your trophy, especially in the midst of a perverted and hostile world.

My children grew up understanding this. They were raised in an environment where the subject of sex was very much in the open. Kathy and I talked candidly about sex with them and tried to demystify it as much as possible in an appropriate way. As our children came into puberty, Kathy and I took them out on dates and talked to them about the high value of their purity. We explained to them that they needed a plan to get their virginity from the battlefield to the honeymoon suite. We told them that they would need the help of Jesus to win this fight, and we offered to lead them into a covenant with Him. A covenant is an agreement made between two parties where both parties have the right and the responsibility to carry out certain commitments to fulfill a desired outcome.

When they felt they were ready, we directed them in a simple prayer of commitment to the Lord, asking Him to keep them pure for the future man or woman of their dreams. They prayed for God to help them in times of weakness, to keep them from temptation, and to impart His wisdom for their life. At the end of the prayer of dedication, Kathy and I gave them each a beautiful ring that they wore on their wedding ring fingers until they were married, as a reminder of the covenant they had made with their God to keep themselves pure. Then, in their wedding ceremonies, they gave their virginity rings to their lovers as a first sign of their covenant with them.

I share this because the lives of my children are testimonies to the power of covenant. God was faithful to them, and He will be faithful to you, too. My kids experienced all the normal struggles everyone goes through in learning to deal with a sex drive, but the wisdom and strength that they gained through their relationships with God enabled them to be successful in managing their desires toward the virtues and goals they had embraced. (There is a cool story in the last chapter of this book about Anthony's covenant ring and his journey toward marriage.)

ACCOUNTABILITY

Another important element in my kids' plans for purity was accountability. After you make this agreement with the Lord about your purity, you need to find someone to hold you accountable for your covenant and your convictions.

There are some very important points to consider in finding the right person to submit to. One of the ways you'll know the right person is to imagine how it would feel to tell him or her about failing to honor your virtues. If you don't have any fear of disappointing that person, then you chose the wrong person. The goal is to become accountable to someone you respect, like a father or mother, not a friend who is struggling with the same issues as you. Of course, this mothering or fathering person needs to be understanding and encouraging, but they should also be someone who will confront you when they see you messing up and call you back to your convictions. It isn't real accountability when you are responsible to people who are "smaller" than you, who are more messed up than you, or who you would have no problem disappointing.

So what does accountability look like? One thing it *doesn't* look like is making another person responsible for your life. You first have to be accountable to yourself for your virtues before you can ask someone else to hold you accountable for them. Otherwise, that person will be trying to get you to behave externally in a way that you have not committed yourself to live internally. This will also lead you to feel controlled and manipulated by your accountability partner.

It is important to realize that whoever has oversight in your life will also have insight into your heart. This is one of the reasons that you have someone else watching over the virtues that you have already committed yourself to keep. An overseer will help remind you of your goals in the midst of your hormonal storms. They will call you to live above lust and passion, and they can be a sounding board when you are making decisions concerning the man or woman of your dreams.

Accountability requires you to *invite*—not tolerate—input, correction, discipline and confrontation into your life, as well as comfort and encouragement. I can't tell you how many times people have asked me to speak into their lives, and later on, when they hear any kind of correction or redirection from me, they punish me for it. Let's face it—it is hard for anyone to hear correction. But if you argue with the person you have asked to give oversight of you, what is the point of inviting him or her into your life? Of course, arguing isn't the only way that we punish people. Punishment comes in all kinds of packages. Sometimes it manifests in people withdrawing affection, giving the silent treatment or pouting. When you engage in this behavior, you are saying to your overseer, "Please don't tell me the truth. I can't handle it."

OVERCOMING DECEPTION

The issue of accountability brings up an important truth that we all need to learn in life: all of us must have someone in our lives in whom we trust *more* than we trust ourselves. Every one of us is susceptible to deception, and the nature of deception is that we don't know it when we are deceived. (If you know that you are deceived, it's not really called deception. It is called the spirit of stupid!) Therefore, when someone tells you that you have a problem in a certain area of your life, it usually doesn't *feel* real. You have to trust what the other person is saying to you more than you trust your feelings if you are going to be delivered from deception.

One of the greatest areas of deception occurs in selecting a life partner. There have been so many times that I have observed people who fall in love with someone who is *not* good for them. The old saying, "Love is blind," is true. But I would like to add, Lust is even blinder, and it is completely deaf! Sometimes people make the stupidest choices when it comes to finding a mate. When your thoughts are ruled by your private parts, you can come to the craziest conclusions, which will affect the rest of your life. That's why it is so important for you to invite people into your life who can help to oversee your romantic relationships and give you some honest feedback. I have already shared with you how much my mother's opinion influenced my values in choosing a wife.

Let me make it clear that I am not talking about submitting yourself to some control freak or allowing someone to treat you like you are a 10-year-old. I am simply saying that we all need someone to help oversee our lives because we often can't see the forest for the trees. Most of the time, these people will simply hold up the mirror of feedback in front our faces and show us how the attributes that we are cultivating in the secret kingdom of our souls are manifesting in our behavior and affecting the people around us.

I have six guys who I have asked to be overseers in my life. A couple of years ago, I was having lunch with them, and I had this great idea. I said to the men, "Let's take our lunch times for the next seven weeks and give each other feedback about the constraints we see in each others' lives that are keeping us from personal greatness. We can start with me." I thought, *What could they possibly find wrong in me? I am a mature leader.* Remember the nature of deception? Well, over the next two hours, my friends took turns telling me about the problems they saw in my life and describing how my behavior was affecting the people around me. I was utterly devastated. I felt like someone had pulled me through a knothole.

I got home late that night and Kathy was already in bed. I dragged myself into bed next to her, still smarting from my friends' commentaries on my life. She stirred a little and then mumbled, "How was your day, Honey?"

Whining, I gave her a short commentary on what they had said to me, expecting her to comfort me. She rolled over toward me, put her hand on my shoulder as if to reassure me, and then said, "Honey, I have been telling you that stuff for years!" Then she rolled over and went back to sleep.

Ouch! I thought. *That was so painful!* But in the months that followed, I sucked it up and began to take action on my friends' input. I have to tell you that I have grown so much over the last couple of years because of their feedback. I guess King Solomon was right when he said, "Faithful are the wounds of a friend" and, as "iron sharpens iron, so one man sharpens another" (Proverbs 27:6,17). It may be obvious, but the wounds of a friend can only come from a friend. Living an accountable lifestyle can be tough at times, so it is important to develop this culture in your life before you need it. This will allow you to have a history of encouragement and trust with those who hold you accountable before they need to correct or redirect you. But if you wait until there is a problem in your life and then look for someone to submit to, it can be hard to take their advice when you haven't yet learned to trust them more than you trust yourself.

DATING AND COURTING

One of the most frequently asked questions about dating or courting is, "What is the difference between dating and courting, and what's the appropriate behavior in a healthy romantic relationship?" Before I answer these questions, let's review the purpose of hanging out together. For some people, the word *dating* has been used to describe something that you do with the opposite sex to have fun and enjoy your single life, and *courting* is what you do when you are in the market for a mate and you are ready to get married. I actually don't mind these distinctions, but I don't think that they are very relevant for today's culture.

If you're dating someone in today's culture, you should have intentions of getting to know him or her for the purpose of marriage. Otherwise, you should just be hanging out as friends. As friends, the rules of war still need to be kept, for very obvious reasons. There should be no romantic gestures like holding hands, putting your arms around each other or kissing. These actions begin to create expectations in the other person that you don't intend to follow through with. In other words, if you are hanging out just to have fun and not to find your soul mate, don't stimulate each other romantically at all. But if you are dating someone, your intentions should be to get to know them to decide if they are the right person for you to marry.

As you learn to live in accountable relationships, it will become natural for you to submit your romantic interactions to leadership in your life. These leaders should also be part of helping you and the person you're dating develop a plan for purity. Here are a few rules of war that should *never* be broken if you really want to survive the sexual battlefield.

Number one, never date or develop a romantic relationship with someone who is not committed to the same virtues that you hold dear. If that person has not decided how he or she feels about premarital sex, then that person has, by default, decided that he or she is not committed to protecting his or her virginity. The war over your virginity is too vicious for you to not be proactive about it. If you fail to plan, you have planned to fail! Obviously, this means that you have to have a conversation with that person about his or her convictions *before* you get into a romantic relationship of any kind.

You may be thinking, *Wow, that would be a hard conversation to have with someone I don't know well.* That's true, but how would you like to find out that that person's convictions are the opposite of yours by having to fight him or her off in some lonely place all by yourself? It happens all the time! For this reason, it's best to date in groups until you feel comfortable with each other. You will learn a lot about someone by the people he or she associates with. Remember, the primary goal of courting/dating/going out is to get to know each other.

Number two, when you do go out alone, have a plan for the date before you leave. Trying to decide what you are going to do after you get in the car is simply not a good plan. Make sure that you know what the plan is and that you have the right to veto it before you get in the car. Guys, this is the place where you apply what you learned in the last chapter. It is your responsibility to keep the princess safe and secure. You have been entrusted with a treasure. It is important that you protect her purity. When you take her out, you *must* have a battle plan. Don't take her to movies that have sex scenes in them or to places that put her in uncomfortable situations. You should never be alone in places where it is convenient to have sex—your bedrooms, in a house alone or parked in a car somewhere all by yourselves. This is just stupid!

APPROPRIATE BEHAVIOR

When you are dating someone, it is important to not violate each other by behaving in ways that stimulate your companion sexually. These boundaries may vary for different people, but if you are going to have an honorable relationship, you must respect the other person's boundaries. For example, if the guy is not stimulated sexually when he kisses but the girl doesn't want to be kissed until she is married, the standard between them has to be *no kissing*. The person with the greatest boundaries must become the standard that both people respect. Otherwise, one person always feels violated and unsafe. But when you protect a person's standards, even though they are not necessary for you to stay pure, it sends them a very strong message: "I respect and honor you. I value what you think, and I will partner with you to keep your integrity intact." This has powerful implications, and it builds a foundation for an amazing marriage, should that person turn out to be the right one.

But let me give you some dating rules that should be kept by everyone, no matter who you are. You should never touch each other's sexual body parts with *any* part of your body (not just the hands) until you are married. This includes the breast, butt, groin, and legs. So, hugging chest to breast is a great way to stimulate your marriage partner sexually, but it sucks if you are trying to hold on to your virginity in a courting relationship. French kissing is also pretty dumb if you are trying to protect each other's purity. When you stick your tongues in each other's mouths, you are simulating intercourse, and you will stimulate each other's sex organs (unless you're dead or something). Your body was created to procreate, so when you do things that turn on all the sexual systems in it, you are telling your body that you are ready to have intercourse. When all of the systems are a *go,* it becomes quite a feat to shut them down without firing a missile, so to speak.

Most of these "rules of war" or guidelines for a plan for purity are really just common sense, but it is amazing how uncommon common sense is when you think you love someone. This is why it is vital that, if possible, you take the time to make a plan for your behavior before you meet someone. I believe that the more time you spend investing in the details of how you want to live and the kind of relationships you want to have, the more clearly you will recognize people around you who have those same goals and the better you will be able to articulate those goals to someone you might be interested in dating.

In the next chapter, we are going to cover how to pursue a relationship in a healthy way. But before we do that, I want you to understand that the guidelines that you just read are not meant to give you an impossible list of things to follow. The goal is to help you learn how to think and act so that you can live a healthy life. We all know that it's possible to do all the right things and still be wrong because your motives are out of alignment. As well, we can convince ourselves that our behavior is acceptable because it is only bending the rules and not breaking them, but if your motives are wrong, or if you are justifying your way out of trouble, you have missed the whole point in having guidelines in your life.

God never gave us rules so that we can live an imprisoned life trapped in the boundaries of what not to do. God set up a path of freedom for all who choose to walk it, a path that takes you out of the bondage of the world and leads you to wholeness, so that all your relationships emanate the qualities of Heaven.

CONSIDER THIS

1. What do you find most confusing or challenging about managing your sex drive? Why is it important to have a plan to preserve your purity?

    _____

    _____

    _____

    _____

    _____

    _____

    _____

    _____

    _____

    _____

2. What proactive steps can you take to protect the purity of your mind?

    _____

    _____

    _____

    _____

    _____

    _____

    _____

    _____

    _____

    _____

    _____

    _____

    _____

3. Memorize Philippians 4:6-9 (you can do it!). How can focusing on these words strengthen your resolve and help you access God's help? Who in your life can you invite to support you in these areas?

_____

_____

_____

_____

_____

_____

_____

_____

_____

4. Why do you think God puts boundaries on sex? How does God's view of sex compare to the view our culture takes? Which one is healthy and satisfying? Why?

_____

_____

_____

_____

_____

_____

_____

_____

_____

_____

_____

Note

1. James Strong, *Strong's Exhaustive Concordance of the Bible* (Peabody, MA: Hendrickson Publishers, 2007), Greek word #573, *haplous*.

5

THE PURSUIT

BY JASON VALLOTTON

From the beginning of time, humankind has laid life and limb on the line in hopes of having just one chance at love's pursuit. For deep in the heart of every man lies a burning desire to be like Prince Phillip who pierced the heart of the sullen dragon with his mighty sword and awakened Sleeping Beauty with a hero's kiss. In the same light, every woman has inside of her a secret longing to be won over by a knight in shining armor and carried away to a land of unending romance and fulfilled desire. Walt Disney did an amazing job of capturing the desires of humanity, each one in its own light, but noticeably absent from Disney's fairytale is all the hard work that goes into creating a happy ending. We are no longer in medieval days where dragons roam the earth looking for a princess to capture and a knight's valor could win a damsel's heart. Unlike the days of knights and princesses, respect and honor have given way to "freedom of choice," where the loudest source of education has come from the mouth of our broken media. This has resulted in intense confusion as our heads are taught one thing but our hearts desperately yearn for another.

It is vitally important that we untangle this web of confusion by understanding the true roles that men and women play in each other's lives as they move toward romance.

READY, SET, GO?

So much of our society has approached dating relationships like a nomad's journey. There's no real starting point or ending point; instead, its appetites, lusts and emotions direct its senseless drifting. And because of this, almost half of all marriages in the United States end in divorce, and most dating relationships leave the participants worse off than when they started.

We all have a desire to let the beauty of a relationship unfold on its own, but the truth is that a relationship is not a flower lying in a field, but rather, it's a garden that has been planned, sown and stewarded unto harvest. Relationships left unplanned and uncultivated will soon be overgrown with weeds that choke out true love. Therefore, the goal of approaching dating proactively is not to plan the adventure right out of the relationship, but rather to cultivate the field of honor and respect so our connections can be free from the weeds of fear and anxiety.

NO MOUNTAIN HIGH ENOUGH

Let's look at dating another way. Imagine with me that you were going with some friends to climb Half Dome in Yosemite National Park, but none of you had ever been rock climbing in your life. Long before you ever arrive at the face of the mountain, there are many things that you would need to know in order to make sure you have an adventure of a lifetime. Without some pretty intense training in rock climbing skills, along with some basic logistical planning to get you there, what was meant to be a great exploit would soon turn into a rocky nightmare. However, by preparing for the exploration before it happens, you are now able to enjoy the thrill of the climb.

Dating relationships are much like rock climbing— they require planning and preparation so that both individuals can enjoy the journey. So before you even take one step into a relationship, you should sit down and ask yourself a few questions: Am I really ready to date? How do I know I'm ready? Is the person I am dating ready to date? There is no sense in being in a relationship that one or both of you are not ready for. Although there is no such thing as a perfect person or flawless plan, there are people who are more prepared than others for a romantic relationship, and there are plans that most often lead to success.

"Okay," you ask, "how do I know that I am really ready for a romantic relationship?" You are ready to date when you can be a benefit to the person you're with no matter what the outcome of the relationship.

Guys, think about what your relationship would look like if you took God's own daughter out on a date. If you're anything like me, there is nothing that I would ever do to hurt her. In fact, I would ensure that when she was with me, she would feel special, appreciated, and protected.

Ladies, the same goes for you when you are dating God's son. You need to make sure that your actions and participation leave him feeling protected and appreciated, regardless of whether or not the relationship goes the distance.

This means you need to be healthy before you date by taking care of your own issues before you focus on someone else. There is no shame in realizing that you have some struggles to take care of personally before moving forward. What you have to remember is that in a relationship, any cracks in your foundation will be magnified and exposed by the pressure of another person standing on the foundation of your life. Often times, these cracks cause pain in the people who are trying to love you. It's a lot like weight lifting. If you are healthy, then lifting weights makes you stronger, but if you are injured, lifting weights will only further the damage to your body. In order to have a healthy body, you must take care of the injury before adding the stress that weight lifting demands. Again, you must be healthy before taking on the weight of responsibility of another person.

If you cannot honestly say that you are in a place to be with someone else and leave them better off no matter what happens in the relationship, then you should take some time with a mentor or counselor to work on those areas that need attention until you are confident that the cracks in your personhood are worked out.

PLAN FOR THE NEXT STEP

Knowing when to take the next step in a relationship should not be left up to the alignment of the stars or something subjective, but there should be proactive steps that include clearly communicated intentions and expectations.

But before you can tell someone that you want to be in a romantic relationship with them, you need to know who you are, and what you are looking for in a relationship. Understanding these two dynamics will help you decide whom to pursue and cause you to be confident about what you bring to the relationship.

Who you are is a compilation of your identity, beliefs, passions, desires, talents and personality traits. Each one of these attributes should be carefully explored and appreciated for their intrinsic value because you will carry these characteristics into every relationship that you will ever be part of. One of the main goals in life is to see these attributes through the eyes of God. Bill Johnson says, "We don't have a right to have a thought in our mind that isn't in the heart of God." The more you know yourself, the more of yourself you are able to give to someone else, and the more secure and confident you will be in a relationship.

There is no perfect set of "wants" that you should pursue in a relationship (there are evil desires that should obviously not be part of our lives at all). But most of what you "should" desire in another person is determined by individual preference. That being said, the more you know and understand your own needs and desires, the better you will be at discovering what you are looking for in a relationship with another person.

Your destiny will be a huge factor in determining what type of person you will need to be with. For example, if you want to be a missionary in the jungles of the Congo, and you choose to be with someone who hates adventure, it doesn't take a genius to figure out that this is a disaster just waiting to happen. In order for a relationship like this to have any chance of success, one of you would have to be willing to sacrifice his or her life's dream for the sake of the relationship, and that usually doesn't go over very well. Finding someone with the same passion and calling in life can create a great partnership. Remember, you are not trying to find someone you can live with—you want to find someone you don't want to live without. Couples with like passions in life have a natural connection that requires less work to keep their relationship healthy.

Another way to help determine what you desire in a partner is to hang around married couples and see how they interact with each other. Pay close attention to the attributes that you admire in them and the ones you don't like. By discovering who you are, where you are going and what attributes you like in others, you should be well on your way to being able to identify what you are looking for when you see it in someone else.

DTR—DEFINE THE RELATIONSHIP

There are fewer letters in this world that usher in the cold weather of reality like these letters can—DTR. If you are unfamiliar with this acronym, it means to Define The Relationship. In my world, DTR is thrown around like LOL is in the texting world. On any given day, you can walk the halls of our school and hear the whispers of how so and so DTR'd over the weekend. Regardless of who is in the room, everyone will know exactly what is being talked about. As cliché as this term has become, it is still useful to the well-being of our environment. DTR is really where the "official" pursuit of any relationship should start. It's the way that each person communicates what his or her intentions and expectations are for the relationship.

Traditionally, human beings have been known to use proverbial signs of endearment to show their interest in one another, from the little girl who pinches the boy on the playground, to the boy who shows off in front of his "crush" by acting like the class clown. *Humankind has always favored romantic communication in the form of illusive signs because of the inherently low risk of rejection.*

The weakness of being illusive is that each person is left with the impossible task of unlocking the secret code of another's mind, or worse yet, the message never gets delivered. Trying to decode someone's "love dance" can be an incredibly complex way to initiate a relationship that is supposed to be built upon trust.

DTR is the right way to get started in a romantic relationship. It takes a little courage, but it isn't rocket science. Basically, it looks like taking him or her out to a quiet place where you can talk and explain where you are at and what your intentions are for the relationship and vice versa. The beautiful thing about this process is that everything is out in the open; there is no hidden code to unlock or mind to read. In this way, we don't create expectations on either side that we can't fulfill.

SLOW AND STEADY WINS THE RACE

Romantic relationships are predicated on the delicate, yet exciting adventure of allowing someone to get past the outward boundaries of our being, so they can see and influence the very core of our hearts. If you've ever watched a doctor perform heart surgery, you understand what I mean by slow and steady wins the race. The skilled surgeon takes his or her time, paying close attention to the smallest details, knowing that too much or too little of one thing can be detrimental to the life of the patient. Now I realize that developing a romantic relationship is not exactly heart surgery, but oddly enough some of the same principles apply whenever you are dealing with someone else's heart: move slowly and steadily, and pay attention to the smallest detail of the relationship. And like a skilled specialist uses a scalpel, trust and peace are the tools of your operation. These tools should dictate the depth of access that you permit in one another's heart. Allowing your emotions, insecurity or your sex drive to determine the level of your heart's connection is a recipe for a failed relationship.

FOUR GUIDELINES FOR DATING

One of the biggest dangers to any new relationship is the instantaneous release of euphoric emotions that turn wise men into drunken poets at a moment's notice. I can't tell you how many times I have seen innocent, headstrong couples end up in a world of pain because they underestimated the driving force of unbridled emotions. Our feelings are a very vital and powerful part of any love relationship. However, they are very poor decision makers. When starting a new relationship, there are four healthy guidelines that will help you keep your head in the midst of the ensuing onslaught of euphoria.

GUIDELINE 1: START APART AND SLOWLY WORK YOUR WAY IN

Our crazy feelings have a way of pushing the pace way beyond what each person can realistically handle. It reminds me of what happened to me when I learned how to drive my first car. As a 15-year-old, learning to drive a car for the first time was quite a thrilling experience. On several occasions I can remember my dad spending the afternoon riding shotgun in our hand-me-down Pontiac 6000, while I navigated the roadways of Weaverville, California. Now as a young man, you can bet that as soon as I sat in the driver's seat and my adrenaline started pumping, the 35 mph road signs meant almost nothing to me. If it were up to me, I would have made a liar out of the speedometer by pegging the needle past the 140 mph mark. However, because my dad is in the car and because he has a better idea of what's healthy for my life, he's able to give me guidelines that allow me to learn how to drive our car in a safe environment, even when I'm under the influence of adrenaline. By obeying the speed limit and my dad's guidelines, the experience of handling responsibility actually enhances my life instead of ending it.

When building a new relationship, the same principles apply. It's really important that each person manages his or her need for speed by starting apart and slowly working closer as trust is built. Each person's trust and commitment level should always dictate the amount of intimacy that each of you gives in the relationship. By respecting this guideline, over time you will slowly become more intimate as trust and commitment builds. All too often we use our intimacy to build connection and relationship instead of allowing the foundation of trust to build our intimacy. If I am going to give you the most sacred and vulnerable piece of me, I better be sure that you know how to handle it before I offer it to you. The beautiful thing about slowly moving together is that the risk of becoming completely heartbroken is dramatically lessened because we are allowing commitment and trust to dictate the pace of our passion.

GUIDELINE 2: COMMUNICATE BEFORE ACTING

Probably the biggest piece of the puzzle missing in most relationships is good communication. Just because you DTR'd once, doesn't mean that all is well. I once heard of a married couple who was in counseling together because the wife was feeling disconnected from her husband. The counselor listened to the wife explain how she did not feel loved by her husband, and how she was not sure if he even cared for her anymore. Upon hearing this, the counselor asked the husband what he had to say about his wife's comments. His response was shocking but maybe all too typical of men. The husband said, "I told her I loved her the day that I married her, and if ever I change my mind, I'll let her know." OUCH! The lack of communication in this relationship has left one person wondering if she is loved by the most important person in her life, creating a major disconnection between them! Wherever communication is lacking, you can be sure that anxiety and fear will move in and drive love out.

Communication is one of the vital organs of any relationship. And without it, there is no hope for a true, intimate connection. When you are just starting out, make sure that you don't take any major steps without first talking through them with your partner. A major step is any decision that is going to involve the other person, from how often you hang out together, to holding hands and kissing or anything else that could possibly violate the needs of the other person. By talking through each step and sharing your needs and desires, you are creating an environment of trust where intimacy can flourish. When each person's needs are valued and protected, trust is built, and where there is trust, there is the opportunity for intimacy to develop.

Another major aspect that communication brings to the table is the ability to set and meet expectations for the relationship. Anytime there is more than one person involved in something, you can be sure that there are expectations that need to be met. Having the right expectations is crucial for the health of both people because any expectation that goes unmet leads to pain. However, in the same fashion, an expectation fulfilled builds trust and connection. Throughout your relationship, the expectation that each of you have for one another is going to change as the relationship matures. So it's vital that both people talk through the expectations that they have of each other, so that the needs of the relationship get met as they go deeper.

GUIDELINE 3: NEVER MAKE A DECISION OF COMMITMENT WHILE UNDER THE INFLUENCE

Allow me to explain. A decision of commitment is any step that is leading you toward a greater level of intimacy. The speed at which two people create intimacy should not be dictated by feelings or immediate wants, rather it should be determined by the level of trust and commitment in the relationship. For example, when you are deciding to hold a girl's hand or use a word like "love," make sure that the relationship is ready for that type of intimacy. Because our emotions are so powerful, oftentimes the decisions that we make while we are "under the influence" are much different from the decisions that we would have made while being "sober."

Making decisions of commitment with a sober mind keeps the relationship from being an emotional rollercoaster and it also drastically lessens the amount of remorse and regret that we experience from making rash choices. Anytime that you are going to take a deeper step of intimacy in a relationship, make sure that wisdom is guiding you in that decision, and not your intoxicating desires.

A really safe way to ensure that your decisions are coming from a sound mind is to sleep on the choices that you are making. Allow me to clarify. When I first started dating, I made a covenant with myself that I wouldn't make any final decisions in the moment. So for me, that meant that if I was out on a date with a girl, regardless of how much I wanted to hold her hand or kiss her, I would wait until I had gone home and slept on it. When I woke up the next day, if I still felt the same way, then I would move forward as long as she was good with it too. I can't tell you how many times that principle has saved me from complete catastrophe, not just in my love life, but in every area of life. Making decisions with a sober mind is the only safe way to live life.

GUIDELINE 4: DON'T LEAVE HOME WITHOUT YOUR PEACE

There are so many factors that play into being a healthy person and living a healthy life. Peace is one of those factors that you just can't leave home without. Many times throughout my life I have found myself in epic battles, fighting for possession of my own peace. These wars do not begin with the sound of a trumpet that warns of the presence of an opposing enemy, nor are there soldiers standing on a battlefield in plain sight, holding shields and spears. This battlefield is in our minds, and the opponent is the deceptive lies that creep in undetected. If you are among the living, you have experienced these battles.

The opponents that we fight manifest themselves in the form of insecurity, anger, loneliness, rejection, self-pity and frustration. And though these feelings are not evil, if left unattended, they will become as destructive as the devil himself. One of the most important things to know about these feelings is that they need immediate attention because they can have so much influence over us. I refer to these feelings as "red flags." Every red flag, whether it is loneliness or insecurity, leaves you extremely vulnerable.

For example, a teenager in a dating relationship who feels insecure and doesn't deal with it before he or she leaves the house, runs a huge risk of trying to fill that need for security with some type of sexual encounter. So the goal here is to recognize red flags and deal with them quickly by meeting the need in a *healthy* way *before* you leave the house.

About three months ago, I awoke up at 7:00 A.M. to find that my brain had already been up and processing for quite some time. As I lay in bed, these thoughts of insecurity rolled through my mind, one by one making themselves known to me. For a second, I thought about just pushing them aside and going back to sleep, hoping that they would somehow just disappear. But the longer I lay there, the more I began to realize that these "sabotagers" were not going to leave peacefully. Insecurity slowly began to take over my entire soul. I had to decide whether to ignore it or battle it out.

As I thought about it, I decided that leaving the house with a starving heart and no peace was probably a really bad idea! And since I had the day off, I decided to spend the better part of three hours laying in my bed, reading my Bible, listening to God, and journaling through what I was feeling. I dedicated myself to winning the war before the day was over. As time passed, I finally uprooted all of the lies that were attached to my insecurity, and my peace returned to me.

Before you leave the house, take a second to see if you have any "red flags" in your heart. If you do, protect yourself and your environment by dealing with them immediately. However, there are times when circumstances just don't allow you to work on your issues right away. In times like these, be acutely aware of how you are feeling and try not to make any major decisions until you can take care of your problem and become healthy again.

GROWING UP

All human beings are born into this world with a set of God-appointed needs that change as we grow older. For example, if you have ever taken care of a baby, you know exactly what I'm talking about. During the first few years of their life, an infant demands all of your attention. Countless hours are spent feeding the baby, filling sippy cups, rocking, kissing, cleaning up, wiping his or her little butt and taking care of every need that has ever been introduced to humankind. Infants are at the dependant stage of life and are completely helpless to meet their own needs.

As children grow older, they eventually mature into adolescence, when they transition from being completely dependent to being independent. In the independent stage of life, their needs begin to change. No longer do they want or need Mom and Dad to wipe their noses or get them dressed in the morning. They now have the need to feel powerful all on their own and capable of taking care of themselves. They need to be free from the "bondage" of having a "helicopter mom" hovering over them all day trying to meet their needs. These are the years when kids build confidence in their ability to solve problems and learn to make good decisions in the presence of adults who can guide them.

As they mature from adolescence into adulthood, they transition from the independent stage of life into the highest level of living, which is interdependence. Interdependence means that I lend my strength to help you become all that you can be, and you lend me your strength to help me become all that I was created to be. Interdependence stems from the fundamental belief that we don't ever have all that we need on our own, but that together, we can accomplish anything. This level of living is so important because there is no way in this life that you can meet your needs without having other people in your life, nor can anyone else meet all of their needs without other people.

However, it is all too common to find people who have never transitioned out of their adolescent mindset into adulthood; therefore, they spend their adult years as islands to themselves trying to become all that they can be on their own. These folks usually live broken and unhealthy lives.

THE GOD FACTOR

Learning how to get our needs met in a healthy way is vital, because when our needs go unmet, we end up in a world of pain. It is important to realize that there are needs that only God can meet and there are needs that people are supposed to fulfill. The challenge is to understand each role so that we can be complete, lacking nothing. God is the main source for direction, protection, comfort, restoration, identity and love. There is no one in this world who can offer us the unchanging security and love that God can. We are amazing because we were made in His image. We are loved because He gave His life for us. We are safe because He holds the world in the palm of His hand. We are comforted because the Holy Spirit (the Comforter) lives inside of us. We are made whole because He provided healing through the cross, and we have a future because as Jeremiah 29:11 says that God's plan is "to give you a future and a hope"!

Anytime you put something or someone else in charge of meeting your needs, you are going to be in trouble. Now, I know what you're thinking: aren't you supposed to feel loved and accepted by other people? There is a difference between being lovable and feeling loved. For example, in a dating relationship, you have a huge need to feel valued and loved by the one you are with. However, you are not loveable because the person you are in a relationship with likes you; you are loveable because of what God says about you and because of how He created you! Now if the other person doesn't value and love you as a person, then the relationship is going nowhere. You can't be with someone who doesn't see you as God sees you . . . it just won't work.

If you take a close look at how man was created, it's really easy to see that men and women were designed to be together in a covenant relationship. In Genesis 2:18 God decides that "It is not good for the man to be alone," so He took a rib from Adam and made a helpmate for him. When you stop and think about it, Adam had a huge, gaping need for intimacy. He needed a companion, a lover and a partner for life. God knew that the only way he could get these needs met was to take something designed to protect his heart (a rib) and form a wife from it.

We were all created to be adored and live in intimate relationships. Without these dynamics happening in our lives, we are like a person who is deficient of iron. We become weak and anemic, starving for the acceptance of someone who knows us deeply. Intimacy is so important because it's how we receive the highest level of love.

When someone knows the good, bad and ugly of your life and still chooses to love you in spite of it all, you experience unconditional acceptance. Some people define intimacy as "in to me you see." People who are afraid of intimacy never really feel loved. They discredit any affection or affirmation that is given to them because they believe that if people really knew them they would reject them. Therefore, they conclude that the only reason people love them is because they don't know who they really are. Intimacy allows God to love us through His people.

DEAR JOHN

The real risk of intimacy is a broken heart. "Dear John, in the next few paragraphs of this letter I am going to hand back all the beautiful pieces of you that were given to me." These are the kind of letters we all fear. Few things in life are as painful as a romantic break-up. In a moment's notice, every memory that used to bring the warm feelings of endearment is instantly turned into a pool of pain. But there is no way to venture into love without facing the risk of heartache. We can actually only be loved to the level that we can be hurt, so risk is part of the process. However, by understanding how to work through a break-up, you will have the confidence to pursue an intimate relationship without fear.

Most people have spent so much time avoiding pain that they have no idea what to do when they encounter it. The most common response is to ignore it and stuff it down deep inside your soul, hoping that somehow, someday, it will all just evaporate. This couldn't be further from the truth!

When working through pain, it's important that we actually acknowledge what we are feeling. By acknowledging what is going on inside us, we find closure for our pain. Matthew 5:4 says, "Blessed are those who mourn, for they shall be comforted!" Without the mourning, there is no comfort for our souls.

Children are born instinctively knowing how to process pain. If you have spent any amount time with them, you know that they shed tears for the slightest hurt. Unlike most adults, they have the unique ability to work through a lot of disappointment. On several occasions, I have witnessed a child feeling rejected by another child, cry about it for a few minutes and by the end of the night, he or she is right back playing with the same kid again. How does that happen? The child mourned over the painful feelings that he or she had inside, received comfort and forgot about it. When working through pain, every hurtful thought should be processed and mourned until you receive comfort. By *not* avoiding it, you will eventually overcome the heartache and be free of the pain.

I have found that some of the best ways to process through pain is to write it out in a journal or to sing about it. Believe it or not, a lot of the music we listen to and enjoy began as someone's process to overcome. We need to be honest with how we feel and why we feel that way, but we don't want to get stuck there. We need to introduce God into the picture. For example, if you feel betrayed, you should write out why you feel that way, mourn over it, think about it, and when you are all done, ask God what He thinks about it. Once you have done that, ask God how He sees the person who you feel betrayed you. By seeing that person through God's eyes, you can connect to the compassion He has for him or her despite what he or she did to you. This is the perfect time to forgive that person for all of the things that you just wrote down. This is the process of forgiveness.

Once the relationship comes to a close and the process begins, it's time to set some new boundaries for your heart! You can prolong your healing process because you fail to protect your heart by exploring your former date's life. It's so tempting to get on Facebook and scroll through your ex-girlfriend/boyfriend's photos while you cry yourself to sleep. If your relationship is over, you have to work her or him out of that place in your heart. What you have to understand is that the exploration of someone creates passion inside of you. When you create passion that can't be fulfilled, you are inducing your soul to have a hope that will only be broken once reality sets in. In order to fully work someone out of your heart, you have to stop your mind from exploring the possibilities of what the relationship could have been, and work through what it wasn't. It's okay to back off from hanging out with that person until your heart has time to heal. There are few things more important than taking care of yourself. If you can't take care of yourself, then you won't be able to take care of others.

Whether you are the damsel in distress or knight in shining armor, Cupid's arrow is bound to find its mark. Love often comes at the most unexpected times; like a downpour on a sunny day, it rarely announces its arrival before it is upon you. But for those who know how to embrace the driving rain, love's downpour is a romantic walk through the park instead of a watery grave. As you continue, far beyond the borders of this book, you need to set your heart's goal on being a steward of all that love encompasses. You must let your passion for purity drive you to take the practical steps of learning how to develop a plan, communicate your heart, and protect the needs of another. It's time to remove the facades of love and incite a sexual revolution.

CONSIDER THIS

1. Think about how you envision a romantic relationship beginning. Why do you think some people rush into relationships? What are the benefits of having a plan for how to approach dating and romance?

_____

_____

_____

_____

_____

_____

_____

_____

_____

2. Why is it important to know yourself and see yourself through God's eyes before beginning a relationship? Why are knowing your goals and dreams important when looking for a relationship with another person?

_____

_____

_____

_____

_____

_____

_____

_____

_____

_____

_____

_____

3. What issues do you need to work through before you are
    ready to day? As you look at the guidelines for dating
    outlined in this chapter, what plan will you create for
    how you are going to approach romantic relationships?

    _____

    _____

    _____

    _____

    _____

    _____

    _____

    _____

    _____

    _____

    _____

    _____

4. How would having God as your main source for direc-
    tion, protection, comfort, restoration, identity and love
    change your life and you relationships?

    _____

    _____

    _____

    _____

    _____

    _____

    _____

    _____

    _____

    _____

    _____

    _____

6

INCITING A SEXUAL REVOLUTION

Many of the wedding customs in the United States have their roots in Jewish traditions. Bridesmaids and grooms-men are one example of this. Historically, a Jewish wedding lasted seven days. A bridal chamber was erected in the midst of the festival, and after the ceremonial vows, the couple entered the chamber to consummate their covenant. The newlyweds had sex for the first time, and then the groom took the sheets from the bed and hung them over the chamber wall for all the guests to see, thus displaying the blood from his bride's broken hymen (some people call this a "cherry"). Then the celebration began. The bride and groom stayed in the chamber for the week while the guests celebrated outside. This is where grooms-men and bridesmaids came in—they waited on the wedding couple in the bridal chamber so that they could have a good time and wouldn't have to come out.

It seems funny to me that, unlike the Jewish culture I just described, which honors sexual relationships in the context of marriage, there is a high level of shame attached to most of the marriage beds in America. There are a lot of reasons why guilt, disgrace and emotional pain reign supreme in American matrimony. Our society has almost totally divorced the issue of sexuality from marriage and family, and thus, more than ever before, people are experiencing a culture that is downright hostile to a biblical view of sex. As a result, the traditional training that many young people received about sex while growing up is simply no match for the tidal wave of propaganda that they face in this worldly culture.

One thing that we all need to realize about this propaganda is that it's not really about sex or lust; it's mostly about money. The greatest promoters of the world's version of sex are actually businessmen who are making billions from it. Because lust sells, they have worked to change our sexual standards in order to increase their customer base. They hate virginity and marriage because it hurts their bottom line, so they do everything in their power to incite the crowd against virgins, purity and covenant relationships. The entertainment and pornography industries seem to be working overtime to intimidate virgins into becoming customers of their global sex machine. They try to make anyone who won't submit to their machine feel at best like a pathetic loser and at worst like a pathological nutcase—someone out of step with the postmodern mindsets of our time. In war, this would be considered a conspiracy, but in business, it is called an aggressive marketing strategy. It never dawns on these people that "screwing anything that walks" is not a sexual revolution or a postmodern mindset. As a matter of fact, this perversion is older than Sodom and Gomorrah.

COURAGEOUS VIRGINS

Virtually every person in our culture has been defrauded through the onslaught of pornography and every other kind of explicit media that is currently saturating our society. The tragedy is that many of the people who get "slimed" by this stuff are plagued by the spirit of shame. It lies to them and tells them that they aren't pure any more. I believe that this sliming is one of the shadows hanging over

American marriages. We need to hear and experience the good news that these lies don't need to stick to us. It's time for those who are living holy and sexually pure lives to come out of the closet and take a stand for righteous living. It's time for courageous, righteous virgins and married couples alike to get tired of these ignorant billionaires shoving their perverted crap down our throats. We must end the tyranny of little children getting raped and teenagers being turned into whores in the name of entertainment, while these sick businessmen laugh all the way to the bank.

PRUDERY IS ANOTHER PERVERSION

One of the main reasons that the pornographers' strategy has succeeded in the past is that righteous people have overreacted against perversion and have made sex a secret or even a dirty act endured for the sake of bearing children. Victorianism is trying to perpetuate its hyper-prudery into society, making it taboo to speak about sex in churches, synagogues, boys and girls clubs or even among families. God forbid that someone would find out what Mom and Dad are doing in their bedroom at night. Isn't it about time that we stop playing into the hands of perverted souls who are lost in their filth and ravished with guilt?

This kind of overreaction to perversion has become another perversion in itself, one that is even further from the truth about sex. In fact, one of the main reasons why many young people are turned off when they hear the purity message and why they succumb to the world's humanist gospel instead is that, to a certain degree, the world is right about sex. The world says that sex is good, fun, natural and healthy, and that is the truth. The problem with the world's sexual gospel is actually that it doesn't affirm sex enough—it underestimates and even denies the power of intercourse, reducing it to a single-dimensional physical experience, and it doesn't understand the ramifications that sex has on the souls and spirits of the people involved. But the world already has the Church beaten when Christians buy into the lie that sex is inherently bad.

It is time that pure, married lovers let young virgins in on the secret beauty of transcendent sexual experiences. Single people need to understand the difference between "screwing" someone and the lifelong sexual adventures of pure lovers who have merged through marriage. These lovers have their spirits intertwined until they become one song, played on the instrument of eternal love and practiced through episodes of timeless devotion. It is in this place that intercourse takes on triune manifestations; spirit, soul and body flow in and out of one another, creating the ultimate river of passionate intimacy. This is true "inner-course."

COVENANT LOVERS

Contrary to popular opinion, God is not a cosmic killjoy. It isn't God who forbids people from understanding sexuality. He openly spoke of sex all through His own Book. As a matter of fact, sex was His idea. He started it all when He said, "be fruitful and multiply" (Genesis 1:28). With these four words, God initiated the sex drive of the entire human race. When God finished creating the world and giving humankind a sex drive, He stepped back and observed it all from a distance. Then He said it was, "very good" (Genesis 1:31). So it isn't God who is a prude.

The way the Manufacturer designed us to have intercourse is very interesting. Let me explain what I mean. God intended sexuality to be expressed solely within the boundaries of the marriage covenant. He did this because the purpose of sex is not merely to give pleasure, but also to create families, as we just saw in His first command to the human race. Evidence for this purpose exists in the very way our bodies were designed. For years, scientists have been bewildered over what purpose the hymen plays in the body of a woman. (The hymen is the membrane at the opening of a woman's vagina that contains blood. It is most often broken the first time a woman has intercourse). It seems to have no physical reason or purpose at all for being there. Furthermore, when it is broken and the blood is spilled, it doesn't ever heal shut again (like every other part of the body does), and it never fills up with blood again.

One day, I realized why the Creator gave women a hymen. He wanted children to be born out of a covenant relationship between a husband and wife. Therefore, He provided the blood so that a blood covenant could be ratified before the children were conceived. Can you see that the very act of sexual intercourse speaks of God's intention for children to come out of the intimacy of the marriage covenant? He could have arranged for reproduction to be carried out in any number of ways, as we observe in nature. But He designed the human race to reproduce through an act that involves pleasure and requires extreme physical closeness. This speaks of God's desire for children to be born from the intimacy and delight shared by a loving husband and wife.

COVENANT

Hopefully by now you are beginning to see that God's version of sex can only happen when it is an expression of something deeper in the heart of a man and woman—covenant love. Marriage is supposed to be the deepest and most binding covenant on the planet because it is a promise to love each other with the same covenant love with which God loves us.

This kind of love leads each partner in the marriage to commit to four primary principles. First, the couple agrees that their marriage should only be broken by the death of one of them. Second, the couple promises that they are willing to live and to die for one another. In other words, the focus of each member of the covenant is, "I'm in this relationship for what I can give to it, not just for what I can get out of it." True covenant love is expressed in a self-less and giving lifestyle. With that pledge, the couple also promises to be completely faithful to each other and to consider their bodies as belonging to each other, as the apostle Paul taught, "The wife does not have authority over her own body, but the husband does; and likewise also the husband does not have authority over his own body, but the wife does" (1 Corinthians 7:4). And finally, people who are in covenant get naked together like Adam and Eve did in the garden. I don't mean that we should necessarily run around the house without any clothes on, but I do mean that we should leave our armor at the door when we get home. We should allow ourselves to be vulnerable, impressionable, teachable and correctable with our spouse; we should be deeply influenced by our lover.

The ancient writings tell us that Adam "knew" Eve and that she conceived and gave birth to Cain and Abel (see Genesis 4:1-2). The Hebrew word meaning "knew" is *yada*. It doesn't mean that Adam had sex with Eve (the Bible assumes that you know that without being told); it means that Cain and Abel were conceived out of a deep personal relationship between Adam and Eve. In other words, the boys were born out of intimacy, not just intercourse. The very presence of our children is supposed to remind us of the covenant love that we share for each other. When children are conceived in love rather than lust, their hearts become tablets on which husbands and wives write their love letters to one another. The outcome of this kind of relationship is that their children are secure and well-adjusted; they have a healthy self-esteem because their folks value them.

Marriage is more than a ceremony. It is the mystery of selfless wonder, the glue of eternal love, and the intercourse of two souls flowing in and out of each other until their finite boundaries give way to infinite, supernatural union with the Creator Himself. You heard me right, when a man and a woman join hearts in true, timeless love, an amazing thing happens; they invite their Eternal Father to join them in becoming a three-cord strand, an unbreakable bond rooted in celestial spheres. Two individuals become a unity. This is a mystery that cannot be explained; it can only be experienced. A prophet named Malachi spoke about the outcome of this mystery long ago. He said that the Creator of the universe is seeking godly offspring (see Malachi 2:15). When intercourse is an act of covenant, the Creator joins with the marriage, and the sexual union becomes an invitation for godly offspring to emerge.

COHABITING

There is a stark contrast between the marriage covenant and cohabiting relationships. People who live together without being married often excuse themselves by saying that marriage is just a piece of paper. But if marriage is just a piece of paper, then why don't they sign it? The truth of the matter is that those who cohabit don't sign marriage certificates because their relationships are not built on the foundation of covenant love but on having their needs met. As a result, they use the fear of abandonment to manipulate their partner in order to get what they want. The unspoken but very clear message of cohabiting is, "I am only in this relationship as long as you please me. The day you don't make me happy, I'm out of here." In other words, people who live together don't want to make an agreement that lasts forever because that would take away the element of insecurity that they use to keep their partner under the pressure to perform.

Those who cohabit find it difficult to make a decision to be committed to someone for life because such a commitment means that they will have very little control over how their partner will treat them in the future. In a covenant relationship, it is easier to make a life-time commitment because we enter the marriage for what we can give to the relationship, and while we can't control what the other person will do, we always have control over our own behavior.

THE JUDAS SPIRIT

I call cohabiting the prime expression of the "Judas spirit" because, at Jesus' going away party, He said to His team, "one of you will betray Me" (John 13:21). None of His guys knew who the backstabber was until Jesus suggested that they make a covenant. That's when Judas decided that he was out of there. Later Judas betrayed Jesus with a kiss because the *Judas spirit always wants intimacy without covenant!*

This Judas spirit is prominent in our culture. It has begun to dominate the mindset of our country and is exemplified in so many ways. For instance, in our society, it has become commonplace for children to be conceived from a one night stand or a brush with passion. Men sleep with women without any thought about fathering the children they are conceiving. We live in a culture that desires intimacy without responsibility and pleasure without commitment.

The Judas spirit also affects the way many people marry. These folks mistake the wedding for the marriage, resulting in two individual lives that never really merge into a holy union. We need to understand that no matter how beautiful the wedding is, it will never take the place of the marriage. It seems crazy to me how much effort some people expend on their wedding and then, a few years later, how much they spend on their divorce. It never seems to occur to them that if they would have spent half that much effort on their marriage, they would have had an amazing life!

A FATHERLESS GENERATION

One of the destructive consequences that the Judas spirit has created in our culture is a scenario very much like that of the kings of old who had multiple wives and concubines. The wives had a covenantal relationship with the king, and as a result, they carried the king's name, and their children had an inheritance. But the king's concubines had no covenantal relationship; thus they did not carry the king's name, and their children had no inheritance. Basically, their kids were fatherless bastards.

Though we live in a democratic society in which the same civil rights are accorded to every citizen, the damage that fatherlessness creates in the life of a child is very real. The inheritance that we receive from our fathers is more than safety, provision and love; it is the inheritance of identity. Children raised without the influence of a father struggle in life in ways that most of them don't even understand, in ways that originate in the fact that their personhood has not been recognized and affirmed by their fathers.

We live in what is probably one of the most fatherless generations in the history of the world. Other cultures and generations have experienced fatherlessness because wars killed off much of the male population, but this American generation is different. We are a fatherless generation because people are choosing promiscuity, cohabitation and divorce rather than covenant relationships. Even people who get married in the United States are often more concerned about making a buck than nurturing a family. It is important for us to understand how the decisions that we make today affect the lives of so many tomorrow.

WAR ZONES

My father died when I was little, and my mom remarried a while later. My mother and stepfather had a child together and named him Kelly. Their marriage disintegrated when Kelly was five years old. After their divorce, Kelly's dad would call about once a month while he was drunk to exercise his visiting rights. He would say, "I'm going to pick up Kelly at five o'clock tonight. Please have him ready." Kelly would be so excited to go see his dad that he would pack early in the morning. A couple hours before his dad was supposed to arrive, he would take his little Superman suitcase and sit out on the front porch. He insisted on waiting outside. He would sit there all day long and late into the night, no matter what the weather was like.

I would finally come out at dusk and say, "Kelly, why don't you come in now? Your dad must not be coming."

He would insist, "My dad is coming. I know he's coming!"

As the hours rolled on, he would huddle up into a little ball and fall asleep on top of his Superman suitcase. I would pick him up and carry him to bed. This pattern continued for years, resulting in deep wounds and a broken heart.

Out of necessity, children who survive in this environment often become independent and rebellious because they have learned that they can't trust people, especially those who have authority over them. There are so many Kellys in the world who are either born outside of covenant or who experience their parents breaking covenant through divorce.

There are also many others who have moms and dads who parent as a hobby or as a side job because they are out chasing "success." When loving relationships are absent in the lives of children, another message is written on their hearts; it is not a letter of love but one of rejection and abandonment. These things are carved into their tender, little hearts through reckless words and lonely nights.

INCITING A REVOLUTION

This carelessness and irresponsibility must stop. There is an old '60s song that says:

> How many deaths will it take till he knows
> That too many people have died?
> The answer, my friend, is blowin' in the wind.
> The answer is blowin' in the wind.[1]

The winds of change are blowing again! It is time to incite a true sexual revolution by discovering, protecting and displaying the pure power and beauty of sex within covenant. The hour has come for us to wake up and realize that all of these broken covenants are destroying an entire generation. Someone has said that if you don't stand for something, you will fall for anything. It is time to take a stand, to win the prize, to bring home the trophy—the trophy of covenant love, supernatural marriage, and a healthy family. The Kellys of the world are waiting on their Superman suitcases, hoping to be rescued from this insanity! Will you become a superhero or just another villain? Heaven and earth are awaiting your answer!

CONSIDER THIS

1. How does our culture present sexual relationships in the context of marriage? How has sexuality been divorced from marriage? What impact has this had on families?

_____

_____

_____

_____

_____

_____

_____

_____

_____

_____

_____

_____

_____

_____

2. In what ways have you been impacted by the culture's efforts to lower sexual standards? How would you rate your courage to take a serious stand for sexual purity? How would your courageous stand impact the people around you?

_____

_____

_____

_____

_____

_____

_____

_____

_____
_____
_____
_____
_____
_____
_____
_____

3. How would reclaiming the beauty of pure, married love start a revolution in the culture? Why is it important to point to God as the one who is at the core of this revolution for restoring pure pleasure in the marriage bed?

_____
_____
_____
_____
_____
_____
_____
_____
_____
_____
_____
_____
_____
_____
_____
_____
_____
_____
_____

4. How can marriage God's way allow you to experience
    authentic intimacy, healthy vulnerability and a strong
    bond of commitment with another person? How do
    counterfeits of godly marriage create an unhealthy en-
    vironment for the adults and children involved?

    _____

    _____

    _____

    _____

    _____

    _____

    _____

    _____

    _____

    _____

    _____

    _____

    _____

    _____

    _____

    _____

    _____

    _____

    _____

    _____

    _____

    _____

Note

1. Bob Dylan, "Blowin' in the Wind," *The Freewheelin' Bob Dylan* (Free Rider
   Music, 1962, 1990).

7

DIVINE ROMANCE

So what is this all about? I mean, what are you doing here on this planet? Why are you alive? Have you ever thought about it? Are you just a celestial mistake or the result of some kind of cosmic burp? Is it true that your great, great, great grandfather was an amoeba? Do you really believe that your distant cousin is dragging his knuckles on some jungle floor somewhere? If you answer yes to any of these questions, there is no need for you to read on in this chapter.

CREATED FOR GOD'S PLEASURE

The Bible says, "In the beginning God *created*" (Genesis 1:1, emphasis added). That's what I believe. God created man in His own image because He wanted eternal companionship. He didn't need our fellowship, but He wanted it. The psalmist put it this way, "For the LORD takes pleasure in His people" (Psalm 149:4). That's right, He actually enjoys us. He doesn't just tolerate us—He celebrates us!

When God originally created humankind, He made them male and female and told them to reproduce, fill the earth, subdue it and rule over its inhabitants (see Genesis 1:27-28). This planet was to be the first of many kingdoms that humanity would rule with Him (see Daniel 7:27). God was grooming us to co-reign eternally with Him. That's why He didn't childproof the Garden.

He planted two trees in the Garden so that Adam and Eve could learn how to make wise choices. Earth was to be the kindergarten of humanity's royal training.

In the next chapter of Genesis, we get some clues about how and why God created humanity the way He did—in order to fulfill our divine destiny to reign with Him:

> Then the Lord God formed man of dust from the ground, and breathed into his nostrils the breath of life; and man became a living being. . . . Then the LORD God said, "It is not good for the man to be alone; I will make him a helper suitable for him." Out of the ground the LORD God formed every beast of the field and every bird of the sky, and brought them to the man to see what he would call them; and whatever the man called a living creature, that was its name. The man gave names to all cattle, and to the birds of the sky, and to every beast of the field, but for Adam there was not found a helper suitable for him. So the LORD God caused a deep sleep to fall upon the man, and he slept; then He took one of his ribs and closed up the flesh at that place. The LORD God fashioned into a woman the rib which He had taken from the man, and He brought her to the man. The man said, "This is now bone of my bones, and flesh of my flesh; she shall be called Woman, because she was taken out of Man." For this reason a man shall leave his father and his mother, and be joined to his wife; and they shall become one flesh (Genesis 2:7,18-24).

What is interesting to note here is that the Bible doesn't say that Adam required a mate in order to reproduce. God stated that Adam was *alone* and he needed a *helper*. In what way was he alone? He was alone because there was a relational void in his heart because God had fashioned him in His image. God is, in Himself, a relationship, an intimate exchange of love and friendship. Unlike everything else in His creation, He made humankind to relate both to Himself and to one another in this loving relationship. Until God made the woman, there was no one in the Garden to whom Adam could relate in the way he related to his God. And in order for Adam to reproduce children who would bear the image of God, as we have seen, the process of reproduction had to be part of an intimate, loving and faithful friendship that mirrored the relationship that God made us to have with Him.

So God solved Adam's loneliness by putting him to sleep and breaking him apart. From then on, Adam would relate to his wife in the same way he related to God—as partners in the work of God—because she completed him in the same way that God did (compare Genesis 2:18 and Psalm 54:4). Man was manufactured with a God receptacle, so to speak, a place for his Creator to plug into his soul and complete the circuit of his life. God perfectly fits man because he was created for God's pleasure and companionship. And when God literally took woman from man's side, He created a similar void that could only be filled by her. Without her, Adam was missing the rest of himself.

You'll notice that the Bible never counts women in a crowd after this. One of the reasons for this could be that God knows that it takes both male and female to make one whole person! This divine version of marriage is at the absolute center of God's heart and will for humankind. Millennia later, He would reveal to His people that their ultimate destiny was to be married eternally to His Son, to be the Bride of Christ.

LIVING SINGLE

The idea that we have been created to experience this completion through marriage has many implications. For one, it implies that singleness is a state that God doesn't intend most people to stay in for their entire lives. The apostle Paul believed that being single was better for the ministry, but he recognized that singleness required a *gift from God* (see 1 Corinthians 7:7). The word *gift* in this passage means a "supernatural endowment from God."[1] It is the same Greek word *gift* as the one that is used for the *gifts of the Spirit* in the book of 1 Corinthians (see 1 Corinthians 12:1). To stay single your entire life will necessitate a special endowment from heaven, because it takes a man and a woman to be a complete person. How do you know if you have received the *gift of singleness* from God? That's simple. You won't have difficulty controlling your sex drive. Paul said that the single life is preferable, but *that "it is better to marry than to burn with passion"* (1 Corinthians 7:9, emphasis added). You are not supposed to be single for your entire life if you burn with passion for sex.

TRUE HELPERS

One of the ways that men and women complete each other is found in God's statement, "It is not good for the man to be alone; I will make him a helper suitable for him" (Genesis 2:18). Some men have redefined the word *helper* to mean "slave." But the word *helper* here is used 19 times in the Bible. Thirteen of these times, it refers to God (see Deuteronomy 33:7,26,29 and Psalm 20:2, 33:20, 70:5, 115:9-11, 121:1, 124:8, 146:5). Only twice does it refer to women (see Genesis 2:18,20). Women were never created to be slaves to men. They were created to relate to men like men relate to their God. I am not talking about men idolizing women either. I simply mean that women were created to be adored by men and that they were designed to fulfill man's desire for romance.

When God said that He would make a suitable helper for Adam, something very interesting was revealed about the genders. The Hebrew word translated "suitable" means "the opposite of."[2] The point is that men and women are *not* the same, despite popular opinion and political correctness. I am not trying to stereotype the genders. I am simply saying that the differences observable in the bodies of men and women are typical of distinctions that lie in the rest of their beings as well. Like our bodies, our natures as men and women were created to complement one another.

I know this is hard for some women to hear because men have oppressed women for generations. Keep in mind, American women couldn't even vote in this country until 1920! To make matters worse, religion has been the tool of choice for much of this oppression, even though the Bible, particularly the New Testament, empowered women more than any other document written in its time. You may cringe when you read this, but it is true. The Bible was written in a day very much like the culture of Afghanistan ten years ago. If you view the Bible from its cultural setting, you'll understand that it revolutionized the role of women and empowered them in society.

When the Bible was written, women were viewed as the property of men, to be used to bear children and keep house. So when its writers made statements like, "Husbands ought also to love their own wives as their own bodies. He who loves his own wife loves himself" (Ephesians 5:28), it was revolutionary. Or consider this one: "You husbands in the same way, live with your wives in an understanding way, as with someone weaker, since she is a woman; and show her honor as a fellow heir of the grace of life, so that your prayers will not be hindered" (1 Peter 3:7). Listen to what Peter is saying: men, you may be stronger than your wives, but you had better honor them as *fellow heirs,* or God won't hear your prayers! Did you get that? God won't listen to your prayers if you don't treat your wife with honor. Women are to be treated with respect and honor, as people who are inheriting the throne along with men.

God never intended wives to submit to husbands who abuse them and treat them like dirt. Wives are called to submit to husbands who adore them and empower them as fellow heirs, people who co-reign together. Leaders who try to convince wives to be subservient punching bags for rage-alcoholics in the name of God need to have their heads examined. I am not advocating divorce here (though that might be necessary in extreme cases). I am simply saying that if Tarzan wants to behave like an animal, he should stay in the jungle by himself until he is fun to be with!

Let me make it clear that men and women are different but *equal.* When God created men and women, He gave them both authority to "rule over . . . every living thing that moves on the earth" (Genesis 1:28). It wasn't until they disobeyed God and were put under the curse on humankind that a power struggle ensued between them. Jesus redeemed us from the curse of Adam and Eve. So the question is: When are we going to start equally empowering women to exercise authority?

THINKING DIFFERENTLY

Men and women think differently. This is metaphorically demonstrated in the way that they were created. Woman was taken from the side of man and created from a rib, something that lies close to the heart. Women tend to think from the heart, intuitively understanding life through a kind of sixth sense. They more easily perceive circumstances and people from root issues and don't often get sidetracked with the facts and statistics that can often derail men. Men, on the other hand, tend to think from the head. They often place a higher value on facts, data, statistics and logic. But if men and women don't understand and value the differences in their perspectives and reasoning, they can devalue one another. Men can often devalue the intuitive, prophetic, and more spiritual dimensions of life, and women can devalue a perspective informed primarily by facts and statistics.

Please understand what I am trying to communicate here. I am not at all trying to dishonor either gender. I know that women and men are equally intelligent. This has been proven over and over in IQ tests. I also understand that women are not illogical or irrational by nature. Nor am I saying that men aren't intuitive or prophetic. I am simply trying to communicate what I have learned from 35 years of marriage and thousands of hours of counseling couples. *Men and women are not the same!* I realize that I will never be elected to any political office after making this statement—I am not trying to run for president. I am, however, trying to help you have great relationships with the opposite sex. Remember, God made us different because we needed suitable helpers. The more we understand and appreciate how we are different, the better we can draw on and receive the help that we need from one another.

When Kathy and I got married, I didn't understand marriage or women at all. I was so ignorant that it wasn't even funny. My mother remarried twice after my father died. My stepfathers created a completely dysfunctional family because they didn't understand family life themselves. Growing up without a healthy model forced my marriage to become a sort of laboratory where ongoing relational experiments were conducted daily. I have several "revelation bumps" on my head that remind me of some failed lab experiments I conducted as a kid in our family's basement. In fact, I went through a season in which I got so many revelation bumps on my forehead that they were going to change my name to "Lumpy." I just had no value for Kathy's opinion, while we were making decisions, when she refused to produce the facts for her conclusions. She would make statements that began like, "I feel like . . . ," "It troubles me that . . . ," "I don't feel good about that . . . ," and so on.

I would respond with questions like, "What is bothering you about this? Why do you feel that way?"

"I don't know," she would often respond. "I just do!"

" 'I just do' isn't a reason," I would argue. "Give me some facts. Tell me one reason why this is a bad decision." Most of the time she would give up trying to convince me that she was right, and I would prevail with my logic and reason.

But what I learned over time, as many of my great decisions began to turn into mistakes, was that her "it feels like" or "this troubles me" were often a lot more accurate than the "facts"! As the years have rolled on, I have learned to invite the rest of me, my other half, my wife, into all of my decisions. And she has learned the same thing. We were made to be together. We are one flesh—a mystery that seems to unfold with time.

SEX IN MARRIAGE

Another major difference between the genders is the way that we approach sex. Men generally have intimacy so that they can have sex. For a man, sex is the pinnacle, the ultimate goal of the marriage bond. Women, on the other hand, generally have sex so that they can have intimacy.

They're wired to want to feel close, cared about and nurtured as the primary expression of their marriage bond.

I think that the only people who don't think this difference matters are the folks who aren't married yet. Understanding the full ramifications of these genetic differences is essential to a great marriage. You see, if you think about it, the reality is that if each person in this situation is going to get what they really want, they will have to put their needs and desires aside and work on loving the other person. This principle runs through all of life. In order to grow in love, you have to give it away. God set it up so that investing selflessly in one another, in the marriage bed as well as in every other aspect of the marriage relationship, is the only way that each partner can receive what he or she needs and desires.

INCUBATE OR CULTIVATE

The Bible says, "The Lord God took the man and put him into the garden of Eden to cultivate it and keep it" (Genesis 2:15). What I observe is that men were created to be cultivators, and women were created to be incubators—they are "womb-men." A husband cultivates the garden of his wife's heart, and she incubates the seeds of life that he plants in her soul. A husband gives his wife sperm. She incubates it and gives him a baby. He buys her a house and she makes it a home. He brings home the bacon and she makes it a meal. A husband speaks gracious words to his wife and she incubates those words and gives him a song! (Let me make it clear again, that I am not trying to stereotype the genders, nor am I trying to limit the scope of either gender's occupation or role. I am simply trying to point out that the way men and women approach life can be quite different at times.)

Once again, the reality of "two becoming one" is that everything that you sow into your relationship comes right back to you. This is why the apostle Paul gives the following advice, as we read earlier:

> So husbands ought to love their own wives as their own bodies. He who loves his own wife loves himself; for no one ever hated his own flesh, but nourishes and cherishes it, just as Christ also does the church. . . and the wife must see to it that she respects her husband (Ephesians 5:28-29,33).

When a husband and wife make it a mutual priority to sow love and respect into their marriage relationship, they cannot fail to reap a rich harvest of blessing in their lives.

CONSIDER THIS

1. According to the Bible, what does God think of you? What needs and desires did He create in you?

_____

_____

_____

_____

_____

_____

_____

_____

_____

_____

_____

2. Whether you eventually marry or not, what are the benefits of preparing yourself for a marriage relationship by establishing your values, nurturing your spiritual life, protecting your purity, and understanding how the opposite sex thinks and feels?

_____

_____

_____

_____

_____

_____

_____

_____

_____

_____

_____

3. Why is it important for you to better understand how the opposite sex thinks and responds in a relationship?

_____

_____

_____

_____

_____

_____

_____

_____

_____

4. How can understanding the differences between men and women enrich your life and your relationships? How would understanding God's creation impact your relationship with Him?

_____

_____

_____

_____

_____

_____

_____

_____

_____

_____

Notes

1. Robert L. Thomas, *New American Standard Exhaustive Concordance* (Nashville, TN: Holman Bible Publishers, 1981), "gift"; Greek word *charisma*.
2. Ibid., "suitable"; Hebrew word *neged*.

8

HOLY AFFECTION OR FATAL ATTRACTION

One day, I entered our church sanctuary and noticed six young ladies standing at the back of the room just hanging out, laughing and talking. As I drew closer, I recognized them as my ministry school students. I thought, *Wow, those girls are so beautiful.* I decided to make my way over to them and tell them how pretty they were. But as I started to walk over to them, a little voice suddenly spoke in my head: "You'd better be careful. What will people think? People will think you are sexualizing those girls! They will not trust your motives. *Caution! Caution! Be careful! Warning! Warning!*"

I started to turn around and go the other way when I heard another voice in my head saying, "You are not sexualizing those girls. Your motives are pure. You have never had sex with anyone except your wife (even in your mind), for more than 37 years. You are a father to them. Your affection for them is holy."

A war raged inside of me; I stood there paralyzed, not sure what I should do. All of a sudden, I had a vision of my two daughters, Jaime and Shannon. Jaime and Shannon are both beautiful young women and have always been best friends. Jaime is 18 months older than Shannon, and they grew up living in the same room together (along with their huge German shepherd, Samson, who used to get into their beds and push them onto the floor). They traveled the world together at 12 and 14, visiting China, Mexico and Russia, as well as several other countries. But when Jaime and Shannon were teenagers, they had very different experiences when it came to dating and interacting with boys. Although they were both very attractive, Shannon got all the dates, and no one *ever* asked Jaime out. If there was some kind of social event going on in our town, five or six guys would invite Shannon to go to it with them, but no one would ask Jaime to go. The phone would ring off the hook for Shannon, and after a while, Jaime refused to answer the phone because the pain of rejection was so great. When the young men would come to the house to pick up Shannon, Jaime would run upstairs, throw herself on her bed, and bawl her eyes out. So I would run upstairs behind her and hold her in my arms. She would bury her head in my chest and say through her tears, "Daddy, what's wrong with me? Is there something wrong with me? Daddy, am I ugly? Daddy, am I pretty?"

I would say, "Jaime, you are sooooo beautiful! You are such an amazing young woman. But God is hiding you until the right man comes along. You'll see. Your prince will come along someday soon. Now, get dressed up. I am taking you on a date!"

She would get all dressed up, and I would take her out and show her a great time. I actually took her on more dates than I took Kathy on in those years. A few years later, Jaime met her prince named Marty, just as I said she would. He is a gentle, loving man—a man worth the wait. He loves God and Jaime and is dedicated to his family. I am very proud of them. They are senior pastors of a thriving church on the coast of California, and they have two great children, Mesha and Micah.

HOLY AFFECTION

As I came out of this vision, I had a revelation. The world is full of Jaimes, beautiful women and handsome men who seem to be hidden for one reason or another. As I realized this, I just stood there with tears welling up in my eyes, wondering how many of them had no daddy at home who could remind them of their beauty during their hidden years. I wondered what would have happened to Jaime if I wasn't there to comfort her in those days. Would she have looked for love in all the wrong places, subjecting herself to the sexual desires of men in order to try and mend her broken heart?

Finally, I couldn't take it anymore, and at that moment, I decided that as long as my heart was pure, I would never let the world dictate my behavior again. I turned around and went back to the place where the girls were standing. "You girls are so beautiful!" I said. "I mean it. You ladies are awesome. I'm so very proud of all of you."

They giggled as if I had embarrassed them a little, but their countenances told the real story. They were beaming as they thanked me for the compliment. Those girls were different from that day on.

PERVERSION

What I realized through this experience is that perversion has an ecosystem that sustains, perpetuates and nurtures itself. As perversion grows in a society, people begin to withhold their affection so that they won't be perceived as sexual predators. As people withhold their affection, a famine of love begins to grow in the land. In a society starving for affection, love-deprived folks begin to lower their sexual standards to obtain some affection. As they break their moral barriers to do this, perversion increases. This, of course, causes even more people to withhold their love, and the beat goes on and on. Thousands of years ago, the wisest king ever born, King Solomon, wrote, "to a famished man any bitter thing is sweet" (Proverbs 27:7). To love-famished people, even perverted affection is better than no love at all.

One of the manifestations of this perverted ecosystem is that, in most of the world, the line between sex and love has become so blurred that people speak of them as if they were the same thing. There is a huge difference between making love and "screwing" someone. *Sex is not directly related to love on any level.* As a matter of fact, saying that sex is love is like saying that because you flew in a plane you're an astronaut. There are several ramifications and manifestations of misunderstanding the difference between sex and love. The most obvious one is that people who have been taught that sex is love think that someone is showing them love when they are having sex with them. If this were even remotely true, whores and prostitutes would be the most loved people on the planet. I shouldn't have to tell you that this isn't true. As Tina Turner sang, "What's love got to do with it?"[1]

HOLY LOVE

Probably the greatest confusion comes from the other end of the spectrum. I am talking about the folks who really do love someone but don't understand that sex and love aren't directly related, so they think that their love relationships must have a sexual component. All kinds of unhealthy relationships grow out of this dynamic. Some parents even molest their children, thinking they are showing them affection. Yes, it gets that weird!

When men love other men or women love other women without understanding the difference between love and sex, they often think that their affection for the same sex makes them a homosexual or a bisexual. What they don't understand is that there is nothing wrong with having a deep love for someone of the same sex. Love doesn't dictate your sexual preference any more than sex can dictate who you love. There is a great biblical example of this in the relationship between Jonathan and David. When Jonathan, who was King Saul's son, met David for the first time, the Bible says, "the soul of Jonathan was knit to the soul of David, and Jonathan loved him as himself" (1 Samuel 18:1). Many years later, Jonathan was killed in battle. When the news was brought to David, he said, "I am distressed for you, my brother Jonathan; you have been very pleasant to me. Your love to me was more wonderful than the love of women" (2 Samuel 1:26).

People who read these verses through the lens of perversion try to say that Jonathan and David had a homosexual relationship. There is not one shred of evidence for that in the Bible or in any historic account of their lives. But some people have confused sex and love in our society and are trying to rewrite history to validate their dysfunctional relationships or warped worldview. A few people have a hard time accepting the fact that Jesus, who is the greatest teacher and example of unconditional love, remained entirely celibate throughout His life. The truth is that Jesus defined and demonstrated love as sacrifice, not as sex.

There are so many good people in our society who have been misled and confused by not understanding the love of God. Some of these folks come up with the silliest ideas to justify their misunderstandings. I heard a guy on television the other day trying to convince people that homosexuality is a normal lifestyle. He said, "Male dogs hump other male dogs. This proves that having sex with the same gender is just a part of Mother Nature's ways." I remember the days when acting like a dog was considered a negative thing. I hope we don't start peeing on our neighbor's trees or pooping in their yards, because dogs do that too. They also smell each other's butts and lick their own private parts. Some people are so ridiculous! Having sex with someone of the same gender is perversion—the wrong version. But it is healthy and normal to love others the way that Jonathan and David loved each other.

HEALTHY SOUL TIES

Another healthy dynamic we see in the relationship between these two godly men was that their souls were "knit" together. There is a lot of talk about "soul ties" in Christian circles today. It should be noted here that there is such a thing as positive soul ties with people other than your marriage partner. I understand that this is hard to hear in the perverted society that we live in, but it is in the Bible. However, you should beware of developing a soul tie with a member of the *opposite sex* when you are married. I have counseled many people over the years who have a closer friendship and bond with someone outside of their marriage than they have with their own spouse. This gets really strange, and in time, it destroys their marriage.

No one should *ever* hold a higher place in your heart than your marriage partner, except Jesus. Marriage actually transcends a mere soul tie because of sex. Through sex, married people become "one flesh." The Bible puts it this way, "For this reason a man shall leave his mother and father and be joined to his wife, and the two shall become one flesh" (Matthew 19:5). People who marry literally become one. This supernatural reality transcends soul ties, as it bonds married couples at the very core of their existence. The apostle Paul called this a *mystery* (see Ephesians 5:31-32). This mystery can't be explained; it can only be experienced.

But the same apostle, who taught us that the marriage bond is a supernatural mystery, also said that having sex with someone creates unhealthy bonds with them. He wrote, "Do you not know that the one who joins himself to a prostitute is one body with her? For He says, 'The two shall become one flesh'" (1 Corinthians 6:16). So, having sex with several people creates mysterious supernatural bonds with them, through which you become connected at the very root of your existence. And through these bonds, the spiritual realities that those people live with, will dramatically affect you. It's a lot like gluing two boards together and then later ripping them apart. On each board is left the broken splinters of what used to be a whole piece of wood. Unhealthy bonds created through emotional or sexual encounters glue the very essence of who you are to other people. Separation from these people leaves you fractured and confused. When you choose purity after living a life of promiscuity, these unhealthy supernatural bonds with others need to be broken. You can be released from these bonds by repenting of your sin. Repentance means asking forgiveness for doing what God told you not to do, and changing your mind about the way you behaved. Next, ask God to return to them all of the parts that you are carrying from the people you had sex with, and ask Him to return yours back to you as well. This will result in you being a whole person again.

Hopefully you can see that there is a distinction between the bond of sex and a soul tie. Both soul ties and sexual bonds can be either healthy or unhealthy. A couple that develops a healthy soul tie and then gets married will probably have a great marriage because their sexual bond will help to strengthen their friendship, and their friendship will make sex an expression of love. But once again, I want to emphasize that you can and should have healthy, nonsexual soul ties with people, whether you are married or not. It is normal to have loving, affectionate friendships with people of the same heart.

CREATING A HEALTHY ECOSYSTEM

The world is crying out for love, and it is looking for it in all the wrong places. Learning to separate love and sex is the beginning of developing a healthy culture of holy affection. Five different times the Bible says, "Greet one another with a holy kiss," or "Greet one another with a kiss of love" (see Romans 16:16; 1 Corinthians 16:20; 2 Corinthians 13:12; 1 Thessalonians 5:26; 1 Peter 5:14). I grew up in a Spanish family. We kissed everyone on the cheek when we greeted each other, whether male, female, young or old. It made no difference to us. Affection was a huge part of our Latin heritage, and it contributed a great deal to our sense of connection as a family.

People are starving for true love that is manifested through an embrace, a holy kiss or reassuring compliments. But for this culture to be restored, we need healthy fathers and mothers to emerge who don't have some strange agenda in the midst of their "holy kiss" or "loving embrace." In other words, we have to have pure hearts, clean motives and healthy minds before we restore holy affection. We must reverse this wave of perversion and move into a culture that is motivated by real love. The Jaimes of the world are waiting for us to get this right. It seems like every time we turn around, we hear of another famous leader who has fallen into sexual sin. We *must* contend for righteous hearts so that we can see our broken, perverted and abused culture restored and reformed.

FATAL ATTRACTION

However, we need to be prepared for something that can happen as we begin to show affection, with pure motives, to people who are *love-starved*. The Bible says that the world cannot bear up "under an unloved woman when she gets a husband" (Proverbs 30:23). Many years ago there was a woman, who I will call Jane, who worked for me in one of my auto parts stores. She drove one of our delivery trucks and was one the best employees we ever had. When we opened a second parts store in another city, Jane and I regularly began to make the hour-long journey there together. I like to sing a lot, and so I would fill the truck's cab with fun songs from the '60s. As we drove back and forth to work that year, I learned a lot about Jane. Her father had sexually abused her. Her husband, having grown up in an unhealthy environment himself, struggled to show her affection. I spent hours counseling and comforting her as we traveled together.

Then one evening after work, my phone rang at home. I answered the phone and discovered that it was Jane on the line.

"Hello Jane. What's up?" I asked.

"I called to say that I know you want me, and I want you too!" She responded shamelessly.

"What the heck are you talking about, Jane?" I asked in utter shock.

"You have been singing me love songs for months, and I just can't take it any longer. We must have each other!" she said, crying on the phone.

"I have no idea what you are talking about, Jane. I have no romantic feelings for you whatsoever! None!" I said in a stern voice.

"You're lying! You are lying to me! I know you want me! I can feel your love for me!" she yelled.

I was stunned! I ran into the front room, grabbed Kathy, and put her on the phone. "Here, tell Kathy what you told me," I said.

She told Kathy that she was sorry but that she and I were in love and that we had to have each other. Kathy talked to her for an hour but never did convince her that she was delusional. The whole thing continued for more than a year and got weirder as time went on. At one point, Jane threatened to kill herself if she couldn't have me. Then she confronted me three more times in public, making a huge scene each time. It was all very embarrassing and really sad too. I lived with a knot in my stomach for more than a year. She was so unpredictable; I kept wondering what she would do next. Thankfully, I had a good reputation and everyone just thought she was a little unstable. The real problem was that Jane had never been loved before. My love for her had overwhelmed her and created an unhealthy bond between us. I had no idea that this was going on in her heart until it was too late. I learned a really good lesson the hard way.

But I wonder how many people have found themselves in bed together over a fatal attraction? There are so many Janes in the world, men and women who are starving for a father's love, a mother's embrace or some brotherly kindness, but they just don't know how to process it when they receive it. People with broken hearts and shattered lives often attach themselves to anyone who shows them attention. As much as they need compassion, we must beware of people like this. They may make us feel like heroes and feed our egos for a while, but they will eventually suck the very life out of us.

These folks need more than love; they need to be healed and delivered. What they require is something that no other person can or should try to give them. It really can only come from their Heavenly Father. Unhealthy people like this often insist on exclusive relationships, which is one of the best ways to discern if you or someone you know is one of them. They are jealous of anyone who is shown affection besides them. And no matter how much attention and affection you give them, it is never enough. They seem to have a hole in the bottom of their feet that drains any love that they do receive.

KEEPING YOUR HEART OPEN

Clearly, learning to love people is no easy task. We must resist the influence in our culture to sexualize our affection and attraction for people. We must learn to discern signs of unhealthiness in people's interactions with us and to develop the capability to set healthy boundaries with them. And finally, when we do encounter people like Jane, we have to resist the desire to protect ourselves by simply avoiding our responsibility to show love to those around us.

Keeping your heart open to love is a lifelong issue. We are all going to experience rejection, disappointment and other expressions of brokenness. But if we allow our broken hearts to fester, leading us to react with suspicion, rejection and coldness, then it won't be too long before we look just like the people who hurt us. We have to learn to run to the Lord so that our capacity to reach out, trust and show affection to people stays intact. It's true that there are many people who have compromised their sexual standards in order to receive affection. But there are also people who may not be living promiscuously but whose hearts are filled with either bitterness or a deep fear of intimacy because their hearts have been broken in the past and they haven't dealt with their pain. They look pure on the outside, but their motives are anything but. If these people do end up getting married, they may be virgins on their wedding nights, but the issues of their hearts will seriously affect the quality of their marriage relationships.

A successful marriage, and all other successful relationships, can only be built upon the foundation of true, unconditional, non-sexual love. This kind of love "bears all things, believes all things, hopes all things, endures all things" (1 Corinthians 13:7). It may be scary to be that vulnerable, but being willing to take that risk is the only way that we can possibly experience the deep affection and intimacy that we were made for.

CONSIDER THIS

1. How can God's love for you affect your self-image—especially in a culture that places higher value on those who date or are considered attractive?

_____

_____

_____

_____

_____

_____

_____

_____

_____

_____

_____

2. How can you speak into the heart of a friend who doubts his or her worth because of a broken heart? How can your encouragement help him or her build and maintain strong moral standards?

_____

_____

_____

_____

_____

_____

_____

_____

_____

_____

_____

3. What is the difference between sex and love? Why can
    this be confusing? How can this confusion result in
    unhealthy relationships? How does sex outside of mar-
    riage affect the marriage bond?

    _____

    _____

    _____

    _____

    _____

    _____

    _____

    _____

    _____

4. People are starving for true love. How can you offer
    them what they really need in Jesus' name? What pre-
    cautions can you take to keep these expressions of love
    pure and appropriate?

    _____

    _____

    _____

    _____

    _____

    _____

    _____

    _____

    _____

    _____

Note

1. Tina Turner, "What's Love Got To Do With It?" *Private Dancer* (Capitol,
   1998, 2000).

9

ON THE EVE OF
DESTRUCTION

It was a cold November day in Atlanta. I had just finished a grueling conference schedule and was eager to get home. I cleared security and boarded the plane, looking forward to the solace of privacy among strangers. I found my row, organized my stuff and finally came to rest in my seat. As I strapped myself in, I smiled warmly at the small-framed, middle-aged man sitting next to me, but I offered him no greeting. He extended his hand and introduced himself. I returned the introduction and shook his hand, hoping that was the end of it. He, however, seemed hungry to connect and pressed me with questions about my occupation and destination.

When he discovered that I was a pastor, he let me know emphatically that he was a *liberal, atheist* Jewish business-man. He seemed surprised when I ignored this apparent invitation to debate with him. I just nodded my head, acknowledging his position. He went on to tell me that his company made orthopedic shoes for people with problems with their feet but that his business had never made money.

"I used to be a business consultant," I replied, hoping that this common ground would ease the stress between us. Thankfully, he was happy to talk about his business, and as we continued to interact, I started outlining a business plan to make his company more profitable. He took a legal pad out of his briefcase and began to take notes. Three hours and ten pages of notes later, my new friend had a detailed strategy for making his failing business profitable. He was so excited that he kept insisting on making some custom shoes for me just to thank me—which was quite a gift at $2,500 a pair.

Then something crazy happened. His countenance changed, as if he suddenly remembered that he was a liberal atheist and felt bad for befriending me. He abruptly asked, "What do think about abortion?" I could feel the tension growing in the plane. I dropped my head, acknowledging that we had very different value systems for our lives. Then I thought of a way to respond to his question.

"You're Jewish, right?" I asked.

"Yes," he said defensively. "I told you I was!"

"Do you know how Hitler persuaded the German people to destroy more than six million of your Jewish ancestors?" The man looked at me expectantly, so I continued. "He convinced them that Jews were not human and then exterminated your people like rats."

I could see that I had his attention, so I went on. "Do you understand how Americans enslaved, tortured and killed millions of Africans? We dehumanized them so our constitution didn't apply to them, and then we treated them worse than animals."

"How about the Native Americans?" I pressed. "Do you have any idea how we managed to hunt Indians like wild animals, drive them out of their own land, burn their villages, rape their women and slaughter their children? Do you have any clue how everyday people turned into cruel murderers?"

My Jewish friend was silent, and his eyes were filling with tears as I made my point. "We made people believe that the Native Americans were wild savages, not real human beings, and then we brutalized them without any conviction of wrongdoing! Now do you understand how we have persuaded mothers to kill their own babies? We took the word *fetus*, which is the Latin word for 'offspring,' and redefined it to dehumanize the unborn. We told mothers, 'That is not really a baby you are carrying in your belly; it is a fetus, tissue that suddenly forms into a human being just seconds before it exits the womb.' In doing so, we were able to assert that, in the issue of abortion, there is only one person's human rights to consider, and then we convinced mothers that disposing of fetal tissue—terminating the lives of their babies—was a woman's right. Our constitution no longer protects the unborn because they are not real people. They are just lifeless blobs of tissue."

By now, tears were flowing down his cheeks. I looked right into his eyes and said, "Your people, the Native Americans and the African Americans should be the greatest defenders of the unborn on the planet. After all, you know what it's like for society to redefine you so that they can destroy your races. But ironically, your races have the highest abortion rates in this country! Somebody is still trying to exterminate your people, and you don't even realize it. The names have changed, but the plot remains the same!"

Finally he couldn't handle it anymore. He blurted out, "I have never heard anything like this before. I am hanging out with the wrong people. I have been deceived!"

BLIND PEOPLE MAKE TERRIBLE TOUR GUIDES

My Jewish friend is not the only one who has been duped into this deception. Our court system is so confused about the origin of life that our Supreme Court judges define what women carry in their womb by how it is terminated. Let me give you an example of what I mean. In 2005, Scott

Peterson murdered his wife, Laci, who was seven months pregnant. The fetus died also, and the same court system that allows women to abort their fetuses even in the third trimester with the argument that it is not really a human being and therefore isn't protected by our Constitution charged Scott Peterson with a *double murder*! Think about it—is there anything else, anywhere else in the entire world, that is defined by the circumstances of its termination rather than the origin of its conception?

For instance, imagine running a vehicle into a wall and then, if you did it on purpose, calling it an iron ore mineral deposit, but if you did it by accident, calling it an automobile. How stupid would it be to classify a vehicle by its termination rather than its conception? But our court system does it every day! The people who need the most protection, because they have no voice and no vote, people like Conner Peterson, are screaming silently as they are terminated in their mothers' wombs.

The injustice continues when we call those who are pro-abortion "pro-choice." The question isn't whether a woman gets to choose, but *when she gets to choose*. In nearly every case, the act of sexual intercourse that resulted in conception was a choice made by a man and a woman, an act of their wills (assault rape pregnancies are extremely rare). But "pro-choice" advocates insist that conception is something that is caught, a disease, something that couldn't be helped. When do the children's wills matter? When do they get to choose?

BABIES ARE BEGINNING TO COME OUT FOR THEMSELVES

On October 24, 2006, the world stood by in utter shock! The story was on the front page of every newspaper in the country, was the subject of every talk show, and was the feature on every news program on television. The event was cited as a stunning discovery, a scientific wonder, and a medical miracle. No, this wasn't a new cure for cancer or alien bodies found in the Arizona desert. This was a fetus that turned into a baby and was born after just 21 weeks and 6 days of gestation! Her name is Amillia Sonja Taylor. At delivery, she was 9.5 inches long and weighed less than 10 ounces. Four months later, Amillia went home with her mom and dad, a healthy baby girl!

Sonja Taylor, Amillia's mother, lied about her baby's gestational age (the baby was conceived in vitro) so that the doctors would intervene and keep the baby alive. Before her birth, the rule of thumb was that babies were not generally viable outside the womb before 24 weeks of gestation.[1] So the question is, how can people watch Amillia on television and still believe that a fetus is not a baby?

Baby Amillia's birth reminds me of a story in the Bible where a rich man died and went to Hades, a place that he didn't even believe existed while he was on the earth, where he was tormented. He had five other brothers who were still living on the earth who didn't believe in Hades either, so he cried out in agony to God, "Please send someone back from the dead to warn my brothers about this place!" But God responded with the astonishing truth. He said, "If they don't believe My Word, they won't believe someone coming back from the dead" (see Luke 16:19-31). Amillia lived when everyone thought it was impossible— she was as good as dead in the eyes of the medical community. If you don't believe that a fetus is a baby after Amillia came from the dead to show us the truth about life, then you have an agenda that is not rational! And like the rich man, I'm afraid that it may be a rude awakening when you discover what is actually real.

RELIGION IS KILLING US

Lying agendas that keep people in denial and deception have been common throughout the ages. In the early 1600s, a scientist named Galileo, through the invention of the telescope, observed that the earth revolved around the sun and not the sun around the earth. The Catholic Church was the political force of that day, and Galileo's scientific discovery was opposed to the Church's theology, so the Pope tried him as a heretic. The Church authorities forced him to renounce his discoveries and placed him under house arrest, where he lived out the last years of his life. Galileo was not allowed to state the obvious because it was politically incorrect.[2] Through a highly developed system of punishment, the Catholic Church of that day relegated the general public to ignorance and lies.

Although religion still rules supreme in the political arena, it is no longer the Catholic Church that defines the political agenda of the post-modern age but the religion of secular humanism. Secular humanism is to our day what the Catholic Church was to Galileo's day. Humanism controls popular thought and, through a highly developed system of punishment, holds the contemporary intellect in ignorance, making it costly to acknowledge the obvious and embrace the observable.

The Catholic Church built huge, beautiful cathedrals where the priests would stand and proclaim their philosophies, molding the minds of their constituents and defining their realty. But in the post-modern era, you don't have to go to church anymore because it comes to you. The television sets of today are the cathedrals of yesterday and the media is the priesthood of secular humanism. With well-defined doctrines and highly aggressive evangelistic crusades, these high priests work to proselytize unbelievers and crucify those who won't convert. You might say, "I don't see the media trying anyone in court as heretics like the Catholics did. We live in a modern world where many different views are welcome. America is the land of free speech." Well, if you believe that, then just try telling someone in the news media that you don't believe that homosexuality is normal or that abortion isn't okay. Or try even suggesting to the media high priest that, although men and woman are equal, they are different. You will discover what Galileo and his contemporaries experienced in their day—intense persecution! As far as secular humanists are concerned, you only have a right to *their* opinion!

HE WHO HAS THE GOLD RULES

Many doctors and scientists (not all of them) have bent to this political pressure and refuse to acknowledge the observable. It's important to note here that scientists who believe in something that is politically incorrect today may not get arrested as they did in Galileo's day. They will, however, be poor for the rest of their lives because the political system controls the funding for most of the scientific community. In other words, being politically incorrect as a scientist is financial suicide! Make no mistake about it; abortion is a 90-*billion*-dollar industry that drives a huge part of our global economy. The Civil War was really fought over this same premise. The southern states didn't want to give up slavery because they had an agricultural economy, and inexpensive slave labor was driving much of it. History does repeat itself!

INVENTION IS SUPPOSED TO LEAD TO INNOVATION

When Galileo perfected the telescope (he didn't actually invent it), a whole new world was discovered. Many previous theories became outdated, and astronomy took a huge step forward, or at least it tried to. Today, the sonogram is to modern medicine what the telescope was to the astronomers of Galileo's age. We can now observe the development of fetuses in the womb and see how they respond to different conditions interjected into their tiny environment. What we have learned about early fetal development through the advent of the sonogram is no less than astounding. It should be completely altering the modern view of abortion because we can now witness with our own eyes the fact that the fetus feels pain and fights for the right to live as it is literally eaten alive by saline solution (acid) that is injected into its mother's womb to abort it. But the extreme political pressure that is being applied by the humanist high priests is keeping us in the dark ages of religious doctrines and holding us to theories that are seriously outdated.

It is absurd that modern science has worked unceasingly to recreate, through artifacts billions of years old, the history of prehistoric creatures and propose a complete account of the ecosystem that existed millions of years ago, while persistently hemming and hawing over asserting the idea that a fetus is a baby. How seriously does the scientific community think we should take them when they try to explain the evolution of man through a process of millions of years, citing what they call "evidence" in the fossil record, carbon dating, chromosome precedent and mathematical equations, while refusing to acknowledge the origin of life in the womb of a woman? If the origin of human life can be so perverted by modern science, it leaves any thinking person wondering how scientific presuppositions affect the rest of their scientific theories.

To date, many modern scientists have not had the courage of Galileo but instead have succumbed to the pressure of the religious humanist agenda and exchanged facts for fallacies and fables. Where are the Galileos of our day? Where are the brave souls with brilliant minds who refuse to let the presuppositions of past generations and political agendas of special interest groups pervert their scientific discoveries? Leading scientists need to break the shackles of this religious spirit and enlighten us about the true origin of human life in the womb of a woman. They need to verify the observable and testify as expert witnesses in the highest courts of our land. The earth *does* revolve around the sun, and a fetus *is* a human being!

In our day, this issue holds an urgency that our scientific forefathers didn't face in Galileo's day. How many people suffered over false suppositions of the earth's orbit? None! But the ramifications of fetus misidentification are killing children at the rate of 89 babies per minute, worldwide. That means that in the time it took you to read this line, two children were killed just because some people don't believe that they are really human beings. Now that is a staggering reality! More children have died at the hands of abortion doctors in this country since *Roe v. Wade* than have died in all the wars put together in American history. And the 90 billion dollar question: *Why?*

MOTHERS HAVE BEEN BRAINWASHED

We lived in the Trinity Alps of California for nearly 20 years. One of the things that we observed while living in the forest is that normally passive animals like deer, squirrels or even birds become vicious when their offspring are in danger. Just put your hand in a squirrel's hole, where her babies are nesting, and you will get a revelation about the maternal instinct of nature.

So what has happened to the maternal instinct in human mothers? When the American laws changed, abortion became legal, but our laws didn't require women to abort their children like the laws in China did. So why did the change in our laws result in 1.5 million abortions a year in the United States? In other words, if our laws are not requiring us to kill our offspring, then why are we? You probably won't be surprised to learn that our nation did not lose its maternal instinct in one year, but it gradually eroded over the last 150 years due to a long process of cultural transformation.

This cultural transformation in America began when our country shifted from the Agricultural Age to the Industrial Age. In the Agricultural Age, children worked in the fields as free labor. The economy encouraged people to have large families. The larger the family was, the wealthier their lineage. (This is the reason why most of our school systems still let our children have three months of summer vacation. The summer vacation tradition is rooted in the Agricultural Age when children worked the fields during the harvest. In those days, if school had run through the harvest season, it would have caused damage to either the economy, if the children weren't allowed to work, or the educational system, if the children weren't able to keep up with their classmates.) But when America moved into the Industrial Age, children went from being a benefit to a burden. They still needed care, but they no longer generated income. The effects of this were really felt in the Second World War when our women had to go to work to support the war effort because America was literally running out of ammunition on the battlefield and our men were busy fighting. As women entered the marketplace on a large scale for the first time, children became a logistical nightmare, and society began an accelerated transition from a maternal to a militaristic culture.

THE ROLE OF WOMEN IN SOCIETY

Another cultural transition that dramatically affected the American view of children was the women's rights movement. I mentioned earlier that women were considered second-class citizens in this country from its inception and didn't even have the right to vote until 1920. But with the advent of women's rights came the redefinition of feminine roles. Because men controlled the value systems of our society, they determined which virtues were held in honor and which were disdained. This resulted in masculine virtues being esteemed while maternal roles were demeaned. Consequently, women gained equal rights, but it was only because they submitted to gender cloning and allowed role distinctions to be classed as stereotyping. Basically men said, "If you want to have the same rights as us, then you need to have the same role as we do."

I often wonder what would have happened if our women had said to their husbands, "I will make you a deal. You stay home with the kids for one month, and I will go to work and do your job." I have a feeling that, at the end of one month, the men would have gladly given our women equal rights without gender cloning. But that is not what happened. When society's maternal value eroded, women felt "trapped" at home raising children while watching other women join men in the adventurous world of the workforce. It wasn't long before children became the stumbling stones of the great adventure, and they were sacrificed on the altar of materialism.

EVOLUTION IS A FACT?

While women were working through their role issues in society, another powerful force was emerging in our country. Darwinism was introduced into our school system for the first time in the early 1960s. Although Darwin's theory of evolution had been around since the mid-1800s, it really gained a foothold in modern thinking during the Sexual Revolution. In my opinion, the Sexual Revolution created the perfect environment for Darwinism to emerge because people were violating their own moral values and were looking for a way to avoid answering to God for the guilt they were experiencing. Charles Darwin gave the world the excuse that they needed to live like hell and not answer to Heaven.

Darwinism basically says that all life, including human life, evolved from the same source over billions of years, and this argument created three important core transitions in our thinking. First, instead of being taught that we were created in the image of God, as people once commonly believed, we were taught that our ancestors were not divine but ape-like. This transformation changed the way that society valued human life because it reduced humanity to smart apes and elevated the animal kingdom to the value of humans. Humans have hunted animals since the beginning of time (see Genesis 9:3), so it is easy to see how this value system affected the way we viewed and treated our own kind. Now we protect animals and kill babies.

Second, the theory of evolution told us that we came about through a series of cosmic accidents that transpired over billions of years, which signifies that there was no divine design, no purpose for which we came about, and no Creator who loved us enough to die for us. Instead, it's just us—all alone on this giant rock we call Earth. The theory of evolution tells us that we are born to die, with no eternity before us and no heaven after us. This philosophy naturally elevates pleasure as the highest goal of life on this godforsaken planet. "Eat, drink, and be merry, for tomorrow we die" is the motto of this mindset. As we view life from this perspective, it is not very hard to understand why our maternal instincts have been degraded. Whether we agree with Darwin or not isn't as important as understanding that his scientific theories have led us to cultural mindsets that have been ultimately destructive to human dignity and are leading to the demise of human life.

But the final and maybe most destructive cultural shift that evolution delivered to our modern society is a single-dimensional view of reality. Darwinism seeks to explain all of creation through the material world, ignoring the soul of man and denying the existence of the spirit realm altogether. Darwin and his proponents disregard the fact that, since the beginning of recorded human history, on every continent in the world and among every people group, men have claimed to witness miracles—hundreds of thousands of miracles and manifestations that defy logic, reason and material explanation.

I have personally observed hundreds of miracles. For example, I have seen tumors, which were the size of baseballs, disappear under the hands of those praying for the afflicted person. I saw a little boy, born with clubfeet, who was healed and took off running for the first time in his life in a miracle service. I was there when a lady, who had lost a kneecap and whose leg had been fused straight after it was crushed in a car accident, received total restoration. Her kneecap and joint literally grew back as an older lady on our ministry team prayed for her 30 feet away from me! If just one of these miracles is real, then science and Darwinism have a great challenge ahead of them. If something can defy the laws of nature, isn't it reasonable to conclude that creation itself could have come into being from the spiritual dimension?

The Bible says that the spirit realm actually transcends the material realm, and this is seen most clearly in the manifestation of miracles because a miracle is by definition anything that operates outside the laws of nature. Although the spirit world is not visible with a telescope or a microscope, the effects of the spirit realm are discernible and observable in the material realm. Jesus put it this way, "The wind blows where it wishes and you hear the sound of it, but do not know where it comes from and where it is going; so is everyone who is born of the Spirit" (John 3:8). The spirit world has a highly developed ecosystem; although different from the visible realm, it is still very prevalent. What we call miracles in this world are actually spiritual realities manifesting in the natural realm. *Miracles are simply the observable result of a superior kingdom being superimposed over inferior territory—a more highly developed ecological system breaking into a descended reality.*

HOW DO MY CHOICES AFFECT MY INNER LIFE?

If miracles really do take place in this world, then God must be real and not just a religious icon who people worship to soothe their consciences. Not only do God and the spirit realm exist, but our actions, attitudes and choices in this realm determine how the superior yet invisible Kingdom relates to us. When we cooperate with the laws of the spirit, people are healed and live happy lives. But when we violate the supernatural laws of the spirit, we wreak havoc in our lives that can't be fixed with an aspirin or a doctor's appointment.

Abortion is a violation of the supernatural laws of the spirit. When you take the life of your unborn child, you invite all kinds of devastation into your heart that can't necessarily be explained in words but that will very much be experienced. This often results in symptoms like sickness, depression, fatigue and a host of other negative conditions that are actually signs of a spiritual storm inside of you. If you don't believe me, do a little research into the post-abortion conditions of most women. Prepare yourself, because what you learn may shock you. You will find yourself wondering why they didn't tell you about this at the abortion clinic. But remember, I warned you that abortion is big business. It is just like selling cars. The clinic only makes money by convincing you to have an abortion, not by talking you out of it.

ON THE EVE OF CONSTRUCTION

The following is the true story of a woman I know who bought into the abortion marketing plan. Jeanine was a typical girl who grew up in an average American family. Her father was an angry man whose verbal abuse and intimidation created a home environment of instability and fear. He unreasonably demanded perfection and nothing that she did was ever good enough. This tension caused Jeanine to live with a lot of anxiety, and consequently, she never bonded with her dad. This, of course, left her hungry for male affirmation and adoration. The vacuum in her soul drove her to search for love and attention in the young men she dated. Her boyfriends seemed to be refuges from the storms of life, safe havens of love and peace.

But Jeanine's intense need for love caused her to develop unhealthy relationships with these men. Soon she became a slave to the men she dated as she struggled to fill the void created by her father. She so feared being rejected by them that she let them violate her boundaries and ravage her purity. This resulted in her becoming pregnant at 17. Her boyfriend didn't want the child, and the presence of the baby threatened to sabotage her relationship with him.

He pressured her to "get rid of it." Twelve weeks pregnant, scared and fearing rejection, Jeanine went to the local Planned Parenthood office to seek advice. It was there that she was told that the fetus she was carrying was just a "blob of cells" and that "the procedure to remove it would take only a few minutes." Single, anxious and alone, she decided to have the "procedure" done.

Jeanine was awake through the entire operation. It was terrifying to hear and feel the doctor remove the fetus from the womb. She was overcome by grief as she left the clinic. "Was the fetus really just a blob, or was it a baby?" she wondered. She struggled to reassure herself that she had done the right thing, but the violence of the vacuum tube probing her abdomen and the sound of it sucking out the pieces of the fetus haunted her. But she needed to please her man and salvage their relationship. Sadly, a few months later, her boyfriend was gone! Grief and guilt became her new taskmasters. She hated herself for what she had done and became bulimic.

Miserable, dejected and despondent, Jeanine struggled to find peace in her soul. Every new boyfriend became a false hope for happiness, another unfulfilled expectation for love. Over the next ten years, she got pregnant four more times by three different men. She terminated each pregnancy with an abortion to preserve the relationship, and yet each of these men eventually left her. Every abortion caused Jeanine to hate herself more. In her last abortion, Jeanine finally witnessed the nature of the procedure that she had submitted to. The image plagued her, contributing to her guilt and self-hatred. Her life became an inner prison; guilt, shame and self-hatred were the bars of her cell, and hopelessness was the ruthless guard. Her maternal instinct evaporated with guilt, and soon she felt completely unworthy of ever being a mother. After all, how could she ever deserve the love of her own child? Shame and remorse caused Jeanine to punish herself. She unconsciously invited men into her life who abused her as a kind of perverted redemption. Although she hated the abuse, it brought her a sense of justice for the things she had done wrong. "After all," she reasoned, "I deserve to be condemned for what I have done to my children."

Thankfully, her story doesn't end there. After more than ten years, five abortions, and numerous sexual relationships, Jeanine reached a point of desperation. She was inspired with a ray of hope when her mother encouraged her to attend a "Bible-believing" church. The next day, a postcard arrived in her mailbox inviting her to a local congregation. It was there, at 30 years old, that she found the wellspring of hope and the door of freedom. The preacher shared the simple message of the redemption that is in Jesus Christ, and that evening she gave her life to Him in a prayer of forgiveness and surrender. In the season that followed, Jeanine learned that the secret of wholeness and peace lay in giving herself to Jesus. He was the only One who had the power to free her from her old life and give her a fresh start.

In the next few years, Jeanine experienced the process of restoration. One day in church, she came up for prayer and was miraculously delivered from bulimia. From there, she joined a group of women recovering from post-abortion syndrome through a program called PACE (Post-Abortion Counseling and Education).[3] This program became the catalyst that the Lord used to complete her healing. A year after Jeanine received the Lord, she found the man of her dreams. They met in church, each in the midst of rebuilding their lives. They have now been happily married for more than 14 years. They have two beautiful children, and life is finally full of laughter and joy. God's redemption has also touched the life of Jeanine's father, resulting in his rededication to and restoration in Christ.

SOMEONE IS STALKING YOU

There is another important reason why Jeanine and so many other American women have been robbed of their maternal instinct. It may be a little hard for some people to grasp, but here it goes. I told you that the spirit world is real and that it has a transcending relationship to the visible world. Well, the truth is that the spirit realm does not merely consist of the superior reality of God's kingdom that is expressed through the miraculous. There is also a dimension of the spirit realm that is expressed, as I just described, in destruction. Within this kingdom of destruction is a serial killer who strikes most often in certain epic seasons of history. In fact, he is not merely a serial killer but a mass murderer who has a history of killing babies by the thousands when particular conditions are present.

His case history reads like a horror movie. The first recorded time he struck *en masse* was in the day of Moses. The Israelites were enslaved by the Egyptian government, and God ordered a child named Moses to be born in order to deliver them from their bondage. Right around the time of Moses' birth, this mass-murdering spirit overpowered the king of Egypt, and he ordered all the male infants to be put to death at birth by the Hebrew midwives. Of course, Moses escaped and 80 years later returned to Egypt to rescue his people. But in the meantime, multiple thousands of babies died.

This spirit's MO was the same in his next human genocide. This time, God's people were in bondage to the Roman government in the natural realm, and they had fallen into spiritual slavery in the unseen world. Again, the people began to cry out for someone to rescue them, and again God sent them a hero in the form of a baby named Jesus. But once more, this serial-killing spirit incited the Roman government against the Jewish people, causing King Herod, who had been installed in Judea by the Roman emperor Augustus, to order all of the male children two years old and under to be slaughtered. Soldiers went from house to house, murdering young babies as their families were forced to watch. Some say that you could hear people weeping and wailing for miles as blood ran down the gutters of the city streets.

Today, once again, people are in bondage and are crying out to be freed from slavery to corruption, addiction and depression, and God is sending us heroes in the form of children. All the conditions have been met for this mass-murdering spirit to be released over our planet. He has followed the same pattern of persuading governments to make decrees while our families stand aside and watch as their offspring are shot with acid and sucked out of their mothers' wombs in tiny pieces, only to be disposed of like common trash! But if history repeats itself one more time, heroes are on the way to deliver us from this insanity and to restore us to our predestined glory.

Will you find yourself on the side of the heroes or standing beside the villains? You might be thinking that you already made your choice long ago when you chose to have an abortion. Well, let me tell you that it is never too late to defect to God's side. He is always ready to forgive and restore you. But you must humble yourself, admit that you were wrong and change your mind about how you view abortion, agreeing with God to value human life enough to never take the life of a baby again. Many people feel sorry for their actions, but they are not willing to change their lifestyles, and therefore, they do not enlist the help of God.

DREAM

Caution! Proceed in this chapter at your own risk! Content contains explicit material that may upset you.

On December 20, 2006, at six in the morning, I had a shocking dream. In this dream, I was sitting next to God on His throne. From the throne we could hear screaming coming from the earth. It was the kind of bloodcurdling screaming that I had heard only once in my life, when a pack of coyotes circled a young doe behind my house in Weaverville in the middle of the night. They ate the doe alive as she screamed for several minutes.

The Father was sitting on His throne holding the earth in His hands. He leaned over it as if to investigate the noise. I became aware that the noise was coming from children in the wombs of their mothers. They were screaming for help as they were being eaten by acid during abortions. Our Father began to weep uncontrollably, and His tears turned to rain that poured over the earth. In the dream, I knew that He was not just grieving for the infants but for the mothers also.

Then, with tears running down His cheeks, He turned and looked deeply into my eyes. I could feel Him staring into my soul, and I could see eternity in His eyes. He spoke to me in a thundering voice, "You must write this book!" The scene changed, and suddenly I was viewing pictures of aborted children in plastic binders on a computer screen. They were gross masses of bloody body parts. I clicked on different ones, and a video of the child's entire life, his or her intended destiny, would begin to play. Then I woke in utter grief.

ON A PERSONAL NOTE

When I began writing this book, I was counseled by some people to leave out this chapter because it would offend a lot of the folks I was trying to reach. But about a third of the way through the process, I had this dream, and I knew that I had to be true to the word that God had given me to share. I don't believe that God is angry with people who have had abortions, but like any loving father, He is terribly grieved that those who have been given a chance at life through no choice of their own, are deciding that they have the right to take that chance away from others.

My mother got pregnant with me out of wedlock in 1954. In those days, society attached a lot more shame to premarital sex than they do now, but I am glad that abortion was illegal and that my mother kept me, even though it was a really hard situation. I had a tough childhood because I was physically and emotionally abused for the first 17 years of my life. Yet God came through for me, and my life has been great. You wouldn't be reading this book if I hadn't been given the chance to live. The Bible says that children are a treasure and a joy, a reward from God (see Psalm 127:3). A lady once asked me, "If God forgave me for having sex outside of marriage when I asked Him to, then why did I still get pregnant?" I told her that the child she was carrying was a sign that God can make something wonderful out of a bad situation!

NO ONE IS UNWANTED

Ladies, no matter how hard life is for you and how tough you might think it will be for the child you may be carrying, everyone deserves a chance. Making your baby die for a mistake that you might have made will not solve your problem; it will only deepen your issues. If a guy tries to pressure you into having an abortion, he is not worth living with! Think about what he is asking you to do and how it will affect the rest of your relationship. He will spend his life making other people pay for the mistakes that he made. Is this someone you want to live with for the rest of your life? You hear a lot in the abortion debate about unwanted pregnancies, but the reality in America is that there is no such thing as an unwanted child. Families are waiting in line to adopt children. There is no disgrace in admitting that you made a mistake and then making a good decision to make it right. Sometimes it is hard to tell people you respect that you are in trouble. But remember, those people have all made mistakes too. If they judge or reject you for your mistakes, it is their problem, not yours. Heaven is always ready to help you. Please—ask.

CONSIDER THIS

1. What value is given to life as portrayed through the media, in your school, in the workplace or in relationships? How do these values affect your value of yourself? Your value of others?

_____

_____

_____

_____

_____

_____

_____

_____

_____

_____

2. How does the culture portray God and His influence in people's lives? What do you think is the foundation for this perspective?

_____

_____

_____

_____

_____

_____

_____

_____

_____

_____

_____

_____

3. How does a view of life that doesn't embrace God's values damage lives—specifically, how is each gender affected? How does it affect your life?

_____

_____

_____

_____

_____

_____

_____

_____

_____

_____

_____

4. What can followers of Christ do to present God's love, redemption and standards for living accurately and positively? Would you have the courage to influence your peers and community in this way?

_____

_____

_____

_____

_____

_____

_____

_____

_____

_____

_____

_____

Notes

1. Amanda Cable, "The Tiniest Survivor: How the 'Miracle' Baby Born Two Weeks Before the Legal Abortion Limit Clung to Life Against All Odds," Associated Press, February 20, 2007. http://www.dailymail.co.uk/femail/article-1021034/The-tiniest-survivor-How-miracle-baby-born-weeks-legal-abortion-limit-clung-life-odds.html.

2. "Galileo's Battle for the Heavens," *NOVA*, originally aired October 29, 2002, on PBS. http://www.pbs.org/wgbh/nova/ancient/galileo-battle-for-the-heavens.html.

3. The PACE workbook that Jeanine used is called *Forgiven and Set Free: A Post-Abortion Bible Study For Women* by Linda Cochran and Kathy Jones (Grand Rapids, MI: Baker Publishing Group, 1996).

10

GRACE

It all began late one summer night years ago when I was taking one of my spiritual sons home after playing basketball with a bunch of teenagers at an old gym in a nearby community. Anthony was unusually quiet as we drove down the winding country road that winds its way through the Trinity Alps. I could tell something was bothering him, but I decided to let him work it out for himself. I knew him well enough to know that he would ask for help when he was good and ready.

Finally, after several minutes passed, he looked over at me and blurted out, "Will I ever fall in love with someone?" Hanging his head and choking back tears, he continued, "All my friends are going out with girls . . . they all seem to be girl crazy. I like girls a lot, but I have never fallen in love with anyone. Is there something wrong with me?"

"No," I responded, "Love happens to all of us, and it will happen to you too. When you are ready, the right woman will come along. You are only 16 years old, and you have your whole life ahead of you, son. Be patient with yourself. You'll see. A woman will show up one day and sweep you off your feet. No worries."

He nodded his head in agreement, but he didn't seem totally convinced. When we finally arrived at his house, he got out of the truck and hurried inside. A piece of my heart went with him as I pondered our conversation and recalled my own struggles with love as a young man. In the days that followed, he seemed withdrawn, contemplative, and a little troubled. When I tried to bring up the subject again, he didn't seem open to talking about it. Days turned into months as summer retreated and gave way to autumn, and finally, winter was upon us.

Then one night the silence was broken by the sound of a knock at our front door. The noise woke me up from a deep sleep. Rolling over, I glanced at the alarm clock and saw that it was one o'clock in the morning. I got up and made my way through the dark living room to the front door.

"Who is it?" I asked quietly.

A voice whispered, "Kris, what are you doing?"

I recognized Anthony's voice. "What do you think I'm doing, Anthony? I'm sleeping," I said.

"Can I come in?" he pleaded. "I met her tonight!"

"What the heck are you talking about Anthony? Who did you meet?" I asked, still half asleep.

"I met the woman of my dreams," he said, raising his voice beyond a whisper and talking excitedly.

Still groggy, I opened the door and we made our way into the front room, which was freezing cold. I sat down, shivering. "Okay, tell me again . . . what are you talking about?" I asked, my tone betraying the fact that I was a little uptight about being dragged away from sleep and a warm bed.

"Remember a few months ago when you told me that someday I would meet the right woman and fall in love? Well, I just met the woman of my dreams! She is so beautiful and her name is Grace. I can't wait until you meet her. You are going to love her. She is amazing." Anthony hardly took a breath as he recounted the details to me.

I was just starting to rejoice with him when he continued. "Her mom is a drug addict and her father left the family when she was really young. She is a new follower of Jesus."

Yikes, I thought. *Why couldn't he fall in love with a nice girl from a great family?* I worked to hide my concern. "Wow! She sounds like quite a gal. I look forward to meeting her."

Apparently oblivious to any lack of conviction in my response, he said enthusiastically, "I will bring her over tomorrow!"

The next day, Anthony sort of floated around like he was in a dream. I can't remember ever seeing him so happy. That evening he brought Grace over to our house to meet us. She was stunning. She had long blond hair that flowed gently around her beautiful face, eyes that glistened with life, a smile that lit up the room, and a great figure, tall and thin. She was warm and welcoming and made us feel like she had known us forever. She carried herself like a young princess. Kathy and I were both taken by her kindness. My fears and preconceived ideas about Grace seemed to evaporate in her presence.

In the days that followed, Grace grew to love hanging out with our family, and she was over at our house often. Then one afternoon, we got a phone call that would forever change our lives. There was a female voice weeping uncontrollably on the other end of the line. After a few seconds, I recognized that it was Grace. She was asking if she could come and meet with Kathy and me alone. Half an hour later, we were sitting on our front room couch holding Grace as she told us her story through her tears.

"I can't marry Anthony!" she said.

"Why?" I asked in surprise.

"Because he is a virgin, and he has saved himself for marriage," she said, hanging her head in shame. "I have slept with many men. Ever since I was a little girl, I watched my mother having sex with men on our living room floor in exchange for drugs. When I was 12 years old, my mom bought me booze and sent me into the bedroom to get laid by a young man for the first time." At this point, Grace was sobbing violently. "The next day, my mom started calling me a slut and a whore," she continued.

As Grace went on to describe her former lifestyle, I couldn't help but think of the girls that I knew in high school who had a reputation as school whores. Those young women had had no sexual boundaries. They slept with anyone who wanted them, and nobody had any respect for them. While I was deeply moved with compassion for Grace, I found myself fighting off panic as I began to imagine Anthony continuing a relationship with this young woman.

Anthony had made a covenant with God when he was 13 years old to save himself for the woman of his dreams. He insisted on wearing a purity ring on his wedding finger to remind himself of his commitment, and he even made a vow to not take the ring off until his honeymoon night. He was so serious about it that he petitioned his coach to get special permission to wear his purity ring when he played sports. However, his commitment to purity had already come through the fire of testing. For nearly a year, he fought an intense battle with pornography that finally ended in victory. I recalled all the days he would talk to me about the war that he was having with shame and guilt as he wrestled with the monster of lust. We would celebrate his victories together and mourn the battles he lost. Anthony's conflict was a family affair because we had made a commitment that, when he got assaulted, Kathy and I would fight for him, encouraging him to not give up but to press through to conquest.

The thought that Anthony was falling in love with a woman who was just now learning what purity was, after all that he had fought for, was a little scary to me. I wondered why this was happening to him—was this relationship really in the heart of God for him or not? Would it be another test that he could pass?

Kathy and I continued to embrace and comfort Grace, who was still weeping. Hopelessness seemed to fill the air as the combined sense of burden for this girl and grief for my son overwhelmed me.

I finally broke the silence. "Let's pray for you, Grace." We all bowed our heads, and I began to pray out loud for her. Suddenly, a thought came into my head, an idea that seemed to be sent from another realm. It startled me, but a ray of hope accompanied the thought. I stopped praying and took Grace's face in my hands. I said, "Grace, I am going to pray for your virginity to be restored!"

She looked stunned; her eyes stared at me in complete disbelief.

I repeated the proclamation again, but this time with more conviction. "Grace, we are going to pray for you, and God is going to restore your virginity!"

"Okay," she said.

With as much confidence as I could muster, I prayed, "God forgives you, Grace, because you confessed your sin. And right now in the name of Jesus, He restores your virginity and your purity."

We didn't hear any angels sing that day. No one wrote "You're forgiven" supernaturally on the wall, and there were no visions of Jesus hanging on a cross for her. But an amazing peace filled us all as we stood to hug each other again. We knew that something had changed.

"Now you have something to fight for," I said, exhorting her.

"Yes," she responded with a twinkle in her eyes and a smile on her face.

As Grace left the house, Kathy and I breathed a sigh of relief. We knew that God had performed a miracle in

Grace, but more than a year would pass before the full revelation of the impact of that prayer would be realized.

Soon after this, Anthony and Grace were engaged to be married. Dating proved to have its own challenges for them. After all, it's pretty normal to want to have sex with the one you love and plan to spend the rest of your life with. However, they also shared the conviction as believers that sex is the consummation that should come after they made a covenant of marriage before God and man. So early on, they developed a plan for purity for themselves, and they asked Kathy and I if we would hold them accountable for the plan. We told them we would, but only under the condition that they would work harder to keep their virginity than we would. They agreed, and we put the plan in motion. We had a code phrase that we would use so that we could check on them without embarrassing them. When Kathy or I would ask them, "How are you guys doing together?" they knew what we really meant was, "How are you guys doing managing your sex drive?" If they answered, "Great," then we knew they were winning the battle. But if they said "okay," that meant that they needed some input from us.

For a while, everything went well. They were clearly working to keep to their plan, and we could tell that Grace especially loved the new feeling of being clean and pure. Then one night something happened. Around midnight, there was a knock on our front door. I opened the door and saw Anthony standing there in the dark.

"What's going on, Anthony?" He fell into my arms and I could tell he had been crying for a while because he was wet with tears. He was now weeping uncontrollably as I tried to comfort him.

"What is it? What's wrong?" I pressed.

"I touched Grace! I felt her breast, and I feel so bad for it."

I looked him in the eye, looking to see if he understood the significance of his confession. "Anthony, you touched the King's daughter. God trusted you with His daughter, and you violated her. I am so disappointed."

"I know, and I feel so bad for failing," he said.

"Well, what are you going to do to clean up your mess?" I asked, emphasizing the fact that protecting Grace and himself was his responsibility.

"I'm not sure yet, but I guess our purity plan is not working," he answered.

"You think?"

The next morning, Anthony and Grace came over, and we talked together for a while. They forgave each other and developed a new plan to secure the battle. This time their plan worked flawlessly. They married a year later with their purity intact.

Anthony had worn his purity ring for several years by the time their wedding approached, but one day, within a week of the wedding, it cracked in half and fell off. They took it as a powerful sign that they had finished the race well.

Their wedding was awesome, and when it was over, the bride and groom were whisked away in a limo to go on their honeymoon. We were so happy and excited for them. Then a couple of days later the phone rang.

"Hello?"

"Hi, Kris," said the voice on the other end.

"Grace, is that you?" I asked nervously.

"Yes, it is."

"What the heck are you doing calling me on your honeymoon? Are you guys doing okay? Is everything going all right?"

"It's going great! I just wanted to call and tell you something. Do you remember when you and Kathy prayed for me? You asked God to give me a fresh start and re-store my virginity?"

"Of course. I will never forget that," I replied.

"Well, God restored my hymen!" she said excitedly.

This was a sign that made our whole family wonder. We were in awe. We had already seen the power of re-demption at work in Anthony and Grace's relationship, and we believed that God had blessed their union and honored them for honoring Him with their lives. But their honeymoon changed our lives as much as theirs be-cause we all found out just how much God cares about purity and how able He is to restore it fully to us when it has been lost.

CLEANING UP YOUR MESS

The story that you have just read is true, only the names have been changed. We wanted tell their story to inspire hope in people who have lived broken lives and who need a miracle. We decided, however, that telling all of the gory details of Grace's sexual encounters with men really wasn't necessary. We all know people like her, and it wouldn't take much imagination to fill in the blanks.

We've seen God duplicate this miracle of restoration in the lives of many other women, and we know that He will do the same for you. You can never fall so far that you can't be restored. Whether you have lived a life like Grace's or you have just failed your own standards, you need to understand how to clean up your mess and get yourself back on the Holy Highway again.

Earlier, I told you that a new life is available to you by simply repenting and asking Jesus to forgive you. What you need to know about forgiveness is that forgiveness restores the standard in our lives.

FORGIVENESS RESTORES THE STANDARD

I learned this lesson years ago when my kids were teen-agers. I became angry with Kathy in front of them and treated her disrespectfully. An hour later, I apologized, and she forgave me. But when I went to bed that night, I suddenly realized that I had disrespected Kathy in front of my teenage kids. So I needed to apologize to them for being a bad example of a husband, or they would grow up believing that my behavior was okay. The next day, I gathered the kids together in the front room and asked Kathy and each of the kids to forgive me.

"Okay, Dad," they each said, a little annoyed that I was making such a big deal out of this. "We forgive you. Can we go now?" they pressed.

"You can go," I responded. I was as glad to get that over with as they were.

About a week later, one of our boys came in the kitchen and started being sarcastic with Kathy. I walked into the kitchen and said, "You don't have permission to talk to my wife like that."

"You were rude to Mom the other day yourself!" he responded.

"Yes," I continued, "but you forgave me. Forgiveness restores the standard. When you forgave me you gave up your right to act the same way that I did because your forgiveness restored me back to the place of honor. I repented. Repentance means to be restored to the pinnacle, the high place."

"I'm sorry, Mom. I should not have spoken to you that way," he said humbly.

"I forgive you, son," she said, embracing him.

If we don't understand this principle, then the lowest point, the worst mistake or stupidest thing that we have ever done in life becomes our high watermark. For instance, if we were immoral as a teenager and later on in life we have teenagers, we won't have confidence to correct them for their poor sexual choices because we failed ourselves. Failures that we have repented of are no longer the standard that we must bow to. When we asked God and those we had hurt to forgive us, we were set back up on the high place that God assigned to us. The truth is that forgiveness restores the standard of holiness in us and through us.

When you repent, you have permission to live happily ever after! That's God's gift to you. It's called mercy and grace. Mercy means that you don't receive the punishment you deserve, but grace means that you do receive the blessing you didn't earn. This was all paid for when Jesus died on the cross. Jesus didn't just die *for* you, He died *as* you. You get to live as if you had never failed!

I was teaching this principle at a YWAM (Youth With A Mission) base some years ago when suddenly a young, beautiful woman stood up and shouted, "You are wrong!" Then she just stood there weeping out loud.

"What do you mean 'I'm 'wrong?'" I asked.

"I have VD because I slept with many men before I started following Jesus," she said through her tears. "How can I live happily after that? Who is going to want me now?"

"When you asked for forgiveness, you received the right to be healed of all of your diseases," I said confidently.

"I don't deserve to be healed because I knew my lifestyle was wrong when I was living immorally, but I did it anyway," she said in a harsh tone of voice.

"Jesus didn't die for your mistakes, He died for your sins," I argued. "Sin means *you did it on purpose*. You can't sin by accident because sin is always a heart issue. Accidents are not heart issues because an accident isn't something you tried to do on purpose. So accidents don't need to be forgiven by God, only things you did on purpose need God's forgiveness. Furthermore, the prophet Isaiah said that Jesus was crucified for our sins but that He was beaten for our healing (see Isaiah 53:5). So Jesus paid the price for us to be forgiven and healed. Why not get all that He paid for?" I contended. "And oh, by the way, none of us deserve anything from God. But we don't get what we deserve. We get what He deserves."

After debating for a while, she finally let God heal her! He is so amazing!

CONDEMNATION AND CONVICTION

When we mess up in life, it is normal and healthy for us to feel bad about what we did until we repent and ask for forgiveness. There are two different reasons that we feel a sense of remorse over our sin; one is healthy and the other is destructive. The destructive sense of remorse is called condemnation. *Condemnation* equates your bad actions with your person. Condemnation says, "You lied, therefore you must be a liar. You slept with someone, so you are a whore. You got drunk, so you're an alcoholic." The goal of condemnation is to convince you that your bad actions are coming from your nature. Condemnation is from Satan and his cronies. He is called the accuser of the brethren (see Revelation 12:10). Once he convinces you that your identity is your behavior, then he can leave you alone because you will always act out who you *think* you are. It is important to understand that you are a human *being* before you are a human *doing!* Therefore, if you believe you are an alcoholic, you will need 12 steps of discipline and a team of people around you holding you accountable for your behavior so that you don't act out your false identity.

On the other hand, there is a healthy sense of remorse that is called conviction. *Conviction* is from God. The difference between condemnation and conviction is that condemnation says, "You sinned therefore you must be a sinner." But conviction says, "You're way too awesome to be acting like that." Conviction separates your bad actions from your personhood and reminds you that you are better than you are behaving. You can tell which one you are under because condemnation makes you feel bad for doing wrong, but it also makes you feel powerless to change. Conviction releases grace on you to change and fills you with hope that things will be different as soon as you repent.

Have nothing to do with condemnation! It will destroy your life. Condemnation is rooted in guilt, shame and punishment. God doesn't do guilt, shame or punishment. Jesus died for our sins so He could set us free from the power of the devil, which is guilt, shame, punishment, depression, fatigue, sickness, death and so on.

There is nothing that you could ever do that could keep you from God's love and forgiveness. There is no life so dark, no sin so shocking, no attitude so bad, no sex so perverted, no relationship so appalling, no pit so deep, no sickness so dreadful that it can't be redeemed by God. He specializes in the *impossible! It's time for you to dream again!*

CONSIDER THIS

1. How can following God's plan draw you closer to Him and help you know Him better? How will this change you for the better?

_____

_____

_____

_____

_____

_____

_____

_____

_____

_____

2. How are forgiveness and second chances part of God's plan to revolutionize the culture? What do you need God to take care of in your life?

_____

_____

_____

_____

_____

_____

_____

_____

_____

_____

_____

_____

_____

3. How does God's grace allow you to enter a godly rela-
    tionship with no regrets—even if your purity has been
    compromised in the past?

    _____

    _____

    _____

    _____

    _____

    _____

    _____

    _____

    _____

    _____

    _____

    _____

    _____

4. With God's forgiveness and grace in your life, what
    standards are you going to live by? How are you going
    to treat others?

    _____

    _____

    _____

    _____

    _____

    _____

    _____

    _____

    _____

    _____

    _____

    _____

    _____

    _____

RECOMMENDED READING

Moral Revolution Audiobook by Kris and Jason Vallotton
(Redding, CA: Kris Vallotton, 2011).
http://store.ibethel.org

*Sex God: Exploring the Endless Connections Between Sexuality
and Spirituality* by Rob Bell
(Grand Rapids, MI: Zondervan, 2008).

*Love and Respect: The Love She Most Desires; the Respect
He Desperately Needs* by Emerson Eggerichs
(Nashville, TN: Thomas Nelson, 2004).

The Five Love Languages: The Secret to a Love that Lasts
by Gary Chapman
(Chicago, IL: Northfield Publishing, 2010).

*Hooked: New Science on How Casual Sex Is Affecting
Our Children* by Joe S. McIlhaney Jr., MD,
and Freda McKissic Bush, MD
(Chicago, IL: Northfield Publishing, 2008).

The Invisible Bond: How to Break Free from Your Sexual Past
by Barbara Wilson
(Colorado Springs, CO: Multnomah Books, 2006).

A L.I.F.E. Guide by Heath B. Wise

Culture of Honor: Sustaining a Supernatural Environment
by Danny Silk
(Shippensburg, PA: Destiny Image, 2009).

*Breaking Free: Understanding Sexual Addiction
and the Healing Power of Jesus* by Russell Willingham
(Downers Grove, IL: InterVarsity Press, 1999).

Falling Forward: The Pursuit of Sexual Purity
by Craig Lockwood
(Kansas City, MO: Desert Stream Ministries, 2000).

*Sex Has a Price Tag: Discussions About Sexuality,
Spirituality and Self-respect*
by Pam Stenzel and Crystal Kirgiss
(Grand Rapids, MI: Zondervan, 2003).

The Supernatural Ways of Royalty, by Kris Vallotton
(Shippensburg, PA: Destiny Image, 2009).

*Strengthening Yourself in the Lord: How to Release
the Hidden Power of God in Your Life*
by Bill Johnson
(Shippensburg, PA: Destiny Image, 2007).

ABOUT THE AUTHOR

KRIS VALLOTTON

Kris Vallotton is the author of several books including the best seller, *The Supernatural Ways of Royalty,* and is a much sought-after international conference speaker.

Kris is the Senior Associate Leader of Bethel Church in Redding, California, and has been part of Bill Johnson's team for more than 34 years. In 1998, Kris co-founded the Bethel School of Supernatural Ministry, which has more than 1,900 full-time students.

Kris is also the founder and president of Moral Revolution Inc. This non-profit organization is dedicated to being a catalyst for another sexual revolution that transforms the way the world views sexuality, defines the unborn and embraces the family.

Kris was a youth pastor for 15 years and he developed a restoration program for juvenile delinquents in Trinity County. This program touched hundreds of teenagers over five years. During those years, Kris won two community awards for his work with young people.

He and his wife Kathy have been happily married since 1975. They have four children and eight grandchildren.

For more information, visit
www.moralrevolution.com

ABOUT THE AUTHOR

JASON VALLOTTON

In 2004, Jason Vallotton became an Associate Pastor at Bethel Church in Redding, California. He is now one of the Senior Overseers of the Bethel School of Supernatural Ministry with a staff of more than 40 people and about 1,900 full-time students.

He is also one of the founding directors and board members of Moral Revolution Inc., a non-profit organization dedicated to being a catalyst for another sexual revolution that transforms the way the world views sexuality, defines the unborn and embraces the family. Jason is a sought-after speaker on moral issues.

He is married to Lauren, and is the father of three amazing young children: Elijah, Rilie and Evan.

For more information, visit
www.moralrevolution.com

ALSO BY
_K_RIS & _J_ASON
VALLOTTON

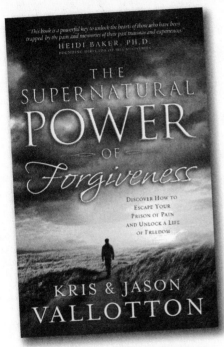

The Supernatural Power of Forgiveness
ISBN-13: 978-0-8307-5737-4
ISBN-10: 0-8307-5737-6

Jason Vallotton thought his world was burning down around him when he discovered that his wife was having an affair and planned to leave him. Using his own story as a poignant, evocative illustration of God's grace and healing, Jason, along with his dad, Kris Vallotton, invites you to reframe your understanding of redemption. Together, they show you how to steward the hardest times and deepest pain of your life so that God can lay a foundation for complete restoration and empowerment for your future. _The Supernatural Power of Forgiveness_ will help you discover that God can not only heal your wounds, but He can also use the healing process to equip you for a whole, fulfilled and powerful life!

"This book is a powerful key to unlock the hearts of those who have been trapped by the pain and memories of their past traumas and experiences."
HEIDI BAKER, Founding Director of Iris Ministries